WITHDRAWN

Sensible Justice

Also by David C. Anderson

Children of Special Value:
Interracial Adoption in America

Crimes of Justice:
Improving the Police, the Courts, the Prisons

Crime and the Politics of Hysteria:
How the Willie Horton Story Changed American Justice

Sensible Justice

Alternatives
to Prison

David C. Anderson

The New Press
New York

Published in the United States by The New Press, New York
Distributed by W.W. Norton & Company, Inc., New York

The New Press was established in 1990 as a not-for-profit alternative to the large, commercial publishing houses currently dominating the book publishing industry. The New Press operates in the public interest rather than for private gain, and is committed to publishing, in innovative ways, works of educational, cultural, and community value that might not normally be commercially viable.

BOOK DESIGN BY ANN ANTOSHAK

PRODUCTION MANAGEMENT BY KIM WAYMER
PRINTED IN THE UNITED STATES OF AMERICA

9 8 7 6 5 4 3 2 1

Publication of *Sensible Justice* was made possible by a generous grant from the Edna McConnell Clark Foundation.

For Betsy

Contents

Acknowledgments

This book was made possible by generous financial support from the Edna McConnell Clark Foundation. Special thanks are owed to Kenneth F. Schoen, until recently head of the foundation's Justice Program, who shaped the original idea and gave unflagging encouragement; to Julie Peterson, Joanne Edgar, and Cynthia Anderson, all of whom provided valuable practical assistance and thoughtful advice; and to Diane Wachtell of The New Press, who combined enthusiasm for the project with shrewd editorial judgment.

Introduction
'Because He Cared'

I MET the man I will call Mal some years ago in the course of reporting about a judge who sentenced young offenders to do odd jobs for public agencies instead of spending time in jail or prison.

Mal was no stranger to the judge. For several years, he had committed burglaries and robberies in order to support his taste for alcohol and drugs. Repeatedly arrested, he repeatedly accepted work assignments. Though he completed them successfully, he then soon returned to substance abuse and crime. The judge, exasperated, finally gave up and sent him to the state penitentiary.

While there, Mal overcame his addictions. Released, he took up carpentry, staid away from alcohol and drugs and became a successful contractor. But he remained a familiar face around the courthouse; I sought him out for an interview as he arrived for one of the rap sessions he conducted weekly with juvenile offenders.

Here is the gist of our conversation, which began when I asked him what he thought of the judge's jobs program:

"Pretty good stuff," Mal said. "It's a good deal for kids. It can work to help kids."

"But did it help you?" I asked.

"Oh, no," Mal replied. "I must have painted the courthouse fence a dozen times. But I kept going back to the booze and drugs. The judge, he finally just got fed up with me and sent me away."

"So how did you get straightened out?"

"I did that by myself. I'd had a wife, and we had a little girl. But after I got sent away she was so mad at me she never wanted to see me again. She left and took my daughter with her. And sitting in prison one day, I realized how much I had lost. I either had to turn myself around or kill myself. And I decided to turn myself around."

"So as far as you were concerned, then, the jobs program here was pretty much a failure."

"Oh, no, not at all. Sure, I rehabilitated myself. But I never forgot how the judge was willing to try to help me all those times. And I think he was trying to help me even when he finally sent me away. That meant an awful lot to me. Because he showed me how much he cared."

I think of Mal whenever I think about rehabilitation: How do people who do wrong turn into people who do right, and who can help them make the change? The question, central to America's discussion of criminal justice for two centuries, continues to torment it. These days, attitudes towards it are rarely positive as politicians responding to public outrage pay more attention to punishment than to reform.

Even so, the idea deserves careful thought. There is substantial history behind it: a belief that man is malleable and that lost souls can be reclaimed shaped the American republic's approach to crime and punishment from the earliest days; it does not deserve to be lightly dismissed. And there are strong positive arguments for continuing to pursue it.

In the 1990's, new police strategies, complementing broader changes in demographics and drug markets, are contributing to big annual declines in crime rates. As they do, they underscore the obvious logic of trying to prevent crime before it occurs rather than assuming that no responses are possible beyond the costly punishment of criminals the system manages to catch and convict. More rehabilitative programs of the sort discussed in the following chapters could powerfully abet the trends already underway. As important, they would leave America in a position to cope more effectively should an increase in the juvenile population or another drug epidemic produce a new wave of criminal violence.

To be sure, the story of rehabilitation in America's prisons, where it began, is too often a story of failure and frustration. Despite the substantial expenditure of money, energy and faith over the years, the goal of locking people up in order to reform their characters remains elusive on any meaningful scale.

Acknowledgment of that in the 1980's constituted a historic change, for prisons had accepted rehabilitation as a primary responsibility ever since the revolution. Americans invented the modern penitentiary as a venue for the proving of rehabilitation theories that had stirred interest in Europe during the 18th century. The hope was that regimens of work and prayer could save miscreant souls and serve as an instructive alternative to the ancient sanctions of torture, mutilation and death.

As penitentiary-based rehabilitation evolved through the 19th century, prison administrators focused on education as well as religion and labor, but produced little in the way of demonstrable results. In the twentieth century, psychologists took over from the educators and preachers. But it eventually became clear that they remained just as empty-handed of therapies that might reliably alter a person's character for the better.

In 1974, a scholar named Robert Martinson published a survey of correctional programs and concluded that "with few isolated exceptions" none had affected recidivism.

Meanwhile, prison crowding and general neglect imposed severe strains on prison management. Wardens felt they were succeeding if they could simply maintain basic control over their institutions; little time or resources were left for reforming character. By the 1980's, it was hard to find anyone, in or out of the standard state penitentiary, who actually believed that the place could do much to alter the personalities and behavior of the inmates for the better.

The discouraging history of prisons stigmatized the whole concept of rehabilitation—and that was unfortunate. For however they might or might not work in prison, there continued to be an important role for rehabilitation programs in the practice of corrections *outside* of prison, a familiar part of criminal justice since the middle of the 19th century.

This was said to have begun in America in 1841, when a kind-hearted Boston boot maker named John Augustus offered to take charge of a drunk who had come before a police court. When Augustus returned the man to court three weeks later, sober and gainfully employed, the judge fined him a penny plus costs and let him go. Augustus began bailing out likely risks regularly; the practice expanded as he was joined by volunteers. "The object of the law is to reform criminals and to prevent crime," he would say, "and not to punish maliciously or from a spirit of revenge."

In 1878, the Massachusetts legislature formalized such release under court supervision, and before long other states followed. By 1940, all states allowed probation release for juvenile offenders, and by 1960 most states had authorized it for some categories of adult criminals. Today it is the most widely imposed criminal sanction: some 3 million convicts are under court supervision, compared with about 1.6 million in prisons and jails.

The system now relies so heavily on probation largely for

practical reasons. It costs about $20,000, on average, to incarcerate a person for a year in a state penitentiary, in a cell that cost $50,000 or more to construct. The average annual cost of supervising an offender in the community ranges from $1,000 to $4,000 depending on the level of supervision. Judges find it hard to ignore such savings when offenders don't pose a serious threat to public safety, or when their youth and vulnerability would guarantee their brutal victimization in prison.

Despite its widespread use, community supervision remains seriously under-resourced; probation officers typically carry caseloads that number in the hundreds—burdens that appear to preclude meaningful control of their clients' behavior. So long as the system remains in place, however, so does its potential. For whatever probation's starved and straitened circumstances, many of its practitioners still feel some responsibility, in the spirit of John Augustus, to help clients address the deeper problems that got them into trouble with the law. And in a few places, given resources and encouragement to think creatively, they are addressing the challenge.

Their efforts may include any or all of several generic elements: substance abuse treatment, community service, private sector employment, academic education, job training, and personal counseling. These are administered under varying levels of scrutiny: strict scheduling of all daytime activity, evening curfews, regular appearances at a central office, regular drug testing, and surprise home visits by probation officers. Offenders may also be required to live in residential drug treatment houses, subjected to electronic monitoring or confined in secure residences. In some programs, they don uniforms and follow a regime that mimics military training.

Thus, for example, in Brooklyn, New York, prosecutors agree to suspend criminal proceedings against drug addicted offenders on condition that they enter residential drug treatment. Cases of those who fail are returned to the district attorney for prosecution.

In Springfield, Massachusetts, offenders sentenced to probation or released early from the county jail are enrolled in a "day
reporting center" where they are helped to find jobs and participate in various kinds of counseling. At first they are subject to
strict curfews enforced by electronic monitors; as they make
progress at work and counseling, they earn more freedom.

In Columbia and Spartanburg, South Carolina, offenders sentenced to pay restitution to their victims are required to live at
secure residences from which they are bused to work each day to
private sector jobs. The faster they earn money, the sooner they
get released. Employers rely on the centers for a steady supply of
workers reliably delivered to the workplace sober, drug free and
motivated to work the graveyard shift so that they can complete
their sentences.

And at a correctional "boot camp" south of Buffalo, New
York, offenders rise before dawn for push-ups and running,
march from place to place in platoons, and line up silently for
meals. In the morning, they are dispatched in work crews to
maintain nearby parks and roads; in the afternoon, they return
to the camp for classes and counseling that follows the routine of
a drug treatment therapeutic community.

In a few places, notably Phoenix, Arizona and the state of
Georgia, probation and corrections agencies have put a number of
programs like these together to create a "ladder" of sanctions,
beginning with standard probation supervision, then escalating
through programs that impose more and more conditions, restrictions and scrutiny. Judges are able to shift offenders from program
to program up and down the ladder as they succeed or fail.

How well do such programs work? Managers of nearly all
can present clients who persuasively say they have gotten the
message; supporters of the programs also point to graduates
who have led stable, law-abiding lives for years. As for hard
research, studies of drug abusers in the 1970's found that significant numbers of those who remained in intensive treatment

programs were drug- and crime-free for several years after completing the therapy. (Whether the same positive results hold true for modern addicts, especially the crack abusers of the late 1980's and early 1990's, remains to be seen.)

Studies of other programs find, most typically, that while they may not reduce an offender's likelihood of recidivating, neither do they increase it beyond the rate for convicts coming out of prison. Such findings buttress the economic argument for probation-based rehabilitative efforts, given the cost saving per offender compared with time in a county jail or state penitentiary.

If there is that much positive to say about rehabilitation out of prison, why doesn't criminal justice make better use of it? Answering that question requires an understanding of recent history.

The years from 1965 to 1975 were eventful in America for a number of reasons: loss of the war in Vietnam, the cultural rebellion of alienated youth, success of the moon landing, the emergence of the environment as a major political and moral issue. A less noted event was easily as important for the country's morale and politics, not to mention the daily lives of millions: Between 1965 and 1975 the nation's murder rate, an indicator of broader criminal violence, nearly doubled, from 5.1 per 100,000 to 9.8 per 100,000.

As a result, pervasive fear of crime, always a familiar aspect of life in poor urban communities, spread out to the middle class. It was the kind of fear that comes into the house: because of it, people spent money they had never had to spend before on locks, alarms and insurance, spawning whole new industries. They gave up use of parks, streets and other public spaces after dark, and sometimes during daylight hours as well. They made elaborate, time consuming plans for the supervision of their children when they were not in school—and in too many places, they even had reason to worry about the safety of children in school.

In the face of this growing anxiety, criminal justice appeared
to have no real answers. Police, lionized by the media as heroic
warriors against chaos, actually remained in a relatively passive
mode. Police managers periodically stung by scandals involving
corruption, brutality and other misconduct, worried as much
about controlling the officers they turned out into the city each
day as they did about controlling crime. They loved innovations
like the radio car, which made it possible for headquarters to
keep in constant touch with officers on patrol, and the 911 system, which required all calls from the citizenry to be recorded at
headquarters before officers could act on them.

But these measures, which gave basic shape to front-line law
enforcement for most of the 20th century, also left police in a
wholly reactive mode, pouring so much of their resources into
rapid response after crime occurs that little was left for trying to
prevent it.

Courts and prosecutors, meanwhile, took a similarly passive
approach to all but high profile cases. In his novel *Bonfire of
the Vanities*, Tom Wolfe accurately described a criminal court in
the Bronx:

> Every year forty thousand people, forty thousand
> incompetents, dimwits, alcoholics, psychopaths,
> knockabouts, good souls driven to some terrible
> terminal anger, and people who could only be
> described as stone evil, were arrested in the
> Bronx. Seven thousand of them were indicted
> and arraigned, and then they entered the maw of
> the criminal justice system.... And to what end?
> The same stupid, dismal, pathetic, horrifying
> crimes were committed day in and day out, all the
> same.... One thing was accomplished for sure.
> The system was fed, and those vans brought in
> the chow.

Practitioners in such courts freely acknowledged that justice had long ago given way to expediency; prosecutors and judges moved along the vast bulk of cases with plea bargains or sentences to "time served"—the few days or weeks the defendant had spent in jail awaiting court action.

Students of criminal justice began comparing it to a funnel. At the top a huge flood of crimes occurred—by the mid-1980's, Federal victimization surveys estimated that 34 million offenses were committed each year nationwide, about 22 million of them "serious" in that they involved violence or significant property loss. Of these only about half were reported to the police, and only about a fifth of those reported resulted in an arrest for a serious crime. More cases fell away as the courts worked through the chow; in the end only a few hundred thousand of the crimes would result in someone being punished by going to state or Federal prison.

This was the situation in 1985, when a new surge of crime began. Drug traffickers' aggressive marketing of crack cocaine in the cities generated violence as dealers competed for territory and addicts sought money for drugs. The crack epidemic, more than previous drug fads, nourished a lucrative market for street guns, which led to an urban arms race. As drug-involved youngsters bought firearms, the streets became more dangerous, prompting yet more youngsters to arm themselves. The resulting increase in gun violence raised the general fear to a new level, along with the belief—abetted from time to time by scholarly research—that government could do little to control crime.

Politicians responded by passing laws designed to put more criminals in prison. They increased sentences for serious crimes and limited the discretion of judges and parole boards to reduce them. This was hardly done out of any surviving belief that prisons could rehabilitate anyone; and though it looked like a way to control crime by incapacitating criminals, that was not really the point either. First and foremost, the lawmakers understood, an anxious public wanted criminal justice to punish—the criminal who inspired fear and disrupted the daily lives of the law abiding should, when caught, be made to feel some fear and suffer other discomforts in return. Whether or not government could reduce crime, it at least could balance the emotional scale. Criminal justice would again, to the dismay of John Augustus, "punish maliciously [and] from a spirit of revenge."

The shift to a criminal justice based on punishment by prison received encouragement from people with narrower interests. The "iron triangle" pushing for longer sentences included Republicans who hoped to attack hesitant Democrats as soft on crime, the prison construction industry, and the National Rifle Association, which tried to deter direct regulation with proposals to increase sentences for crimes committed with guns.

The result was a historically steep increase in the use of prisons to deal with criminals. The number of prisoners in state and Federal penitentiaries had hovered around 200,000 since the 1940's. Between 1975 and 1980, it rose to 300,000, and between 1980 and 1995 it began an astonishing ascent that brought the total behind bars to a solid million. Spending for state prisons rose 359 percent, from 3.4 billion in 1980 to 15.7 billion in 1992. The heavy investment in steel and concrete sapped probation; the percentage of total corrections spending for institutions increased from 80.1 to 83.5 percent, while the total for "other" corrections declined from 19.9 percent to 16.5 percent.

All the prison construction required more than a sizable infusion of capital spending; it also locked in big annual outlays for operating costs. Employees of state correctional agencies more than doubled between 1980 and 1992, from 163,670 to 347,985, though overall employment in the criminal justice system rose only 87.3 percent. That level of spending for corrections caused some people to think harder about what it was actually buying. Politicians weren't about to apologize for responding to emotional public demands for punishment, but what about crime control? Wouldn't it be better, after all, to reduce the source of fear and the ugly emotions it generated rather than allowing them to drive policy? However problematic it had proved to be, wasn't crime control still an important goal to pursue? And what in fact was the punishment-by-prison approach achieving in terms of reduced crime?

On this point, the figures weren't reassuring. Violent crime had declined gradually through the first half of the 1980's as the steep increase in incarcerations began; but from 1985 to 1990, violence, as measured by the national homicide rate, suddenly began to climb in parallel with rising incarceration. Then in 1990, the homicide rate peaked out, even as the incarceration rate continued its increase.

Promoters of the prison-as-punishment response claimed that it had begun to pay off, that the incapacitation of an additional 800,000 people was finally reducing crime. On closer examination, however, that assertion didn't hold up. Beyond the homicide figures, the prison buildup hadn't altered the overall shape of the criminal justice funnel that much. In 1994, even with crime rates turning down, victimization surveys still found about 22 million serious crimes (compared with 1985, the figures showed an increase in violent crimes and a decrease in nonviolent crimes), while judges sent only 541,434 convicts to prison, and about a third of them were nonviolent drug offenders and drunk drivers. A criminal went to prison for only about 1.7 percent of all the serious crimes committed.

Supporters of justice based on prison suggested that increased incarcerations still could be having an effect, since some studies showed that a single convict sent to prison might be responsible for 10 or more crimes per year. But if in fact locking up the additional 800,000 had prevented 8 million crimes per year, why hadn't that been reflected in the crime figures earlier on? Why hadn't violent crime plummeted steadily through the years of steep increases in imprisonment, instead of falling gradually, climbing sharply, then peaking out?

One obvious reason was that releases from prison were increasing almost as fast as new commitments. More prison capacity had made it possible to lock up more people—but it was not sufficient to permit holding them for more than two or three years, on average, even for serious crimes. Thus while 541,434 criminals were sent to prisons in 1994, 456,942 came out, and it is a fair assumption that most of those who came out, unrehabilitated, soon resumed criminal behavior. In effect, the incarceration of a million criminals at a given time in 1994 actually reflected a net incapacitation that year of only 84,492. This does represent an increase over 1980, for example, when 182,617 went in and 169,826 came out, for a net reduction of 12,791. But it is hard to see how expanding the actual number incapacitated by 71,701 (a figure that includes the nonviolent drug offenders and drunk drivers) can have more than a modest effect on the 20 million serious crimes committed in a year, even if many of the 71,701 are likely to commit numerous crimes.

If increased incarceration wasn't the reason for the peaking of violent crime rates in the 1990's, what was? The answers appear to involve events at the top of the funnel rather than the amount of incarceration occurring at the bottom.

Drug epidemics, like disease epidemics, apparently have natural lives. By the early 1990's, drug abusing America's romance with crack cocaine seemed to have entered a final phase, with older addicts dying, seeking treatment or otherwise giving up the drug and few new ones taking their places. Experts speculated about a "little brother" syndrome: as a generation of adolescents allows drugs and violence to destroy their lives, their younger siblings are so traumatized that they vow never to take such risks themselves. At the same time, students of the crack trade found that the violent gangs organized to market the drug in the early days had begun to collapse, riven by internal conflicts or infiltrated and broken up by the police.

But the downturn in crime rates did not result entirely from natural events beyond the reach of organized law enforcement. Dramatic developments in New York and a few other cities suggested another possibility: new police strategies. New York, after years of coping with a police department reduced by a fiscal crisis in the 1970's, finally found money to hire more officers; then a new police commissioner, William Bratton, began rigorous tracking of crime trends in specific areas, aggressive patrols to deal with them, a crackdown on low-level "quality of life" offenses, and strict accountability for precinct commanders. In effect, he shifted the department's strategy from responding to crime to preventing it; his focus on quality of life crimes, in particular, sought to prove out the long debated idea that massive police efforts to control low-level misdemeanor offenses could reduce serious felonies as well.

The results were immediate. New York City's homicide rate rose steadily until 1990, then began a gradual decline, in line with the national trend. But in 1994, after Bratton put his new approach into effect, the decline accelerated steeply. By 1996, only 985 homicides occurred in the city, a drop of 57 percent from the 1990 figure of 2,262. The percentage drop substantially exceeded the national decline in homicides for the same period.

And a few other big cities—notably Houston, Dallas, San Diego and Boston—were showing similar steep declines, all apparently as the result of hiring more police, adopting more proactive strategies or both. The new police activity appeared to complement and greatly enhance the broader forces that had begun to reduce criminal violence. Cities were becoming safer because of events at the top of the funnel where millions of crimes were generated, not at the bottom of the funnel, where a few hundred thousand criminals cycled in and out of prison.

It is against this background that the idea of rehabilitation acquires new relevance. Creative efforts to develop probation-based sanctions for criminals, including substance abuse treat-

ment and other social services, are a logical complement to innovative police work as part of a top-of-the funnel strategy against
crime. They offer judges something constructive and potentially
rehabilitative to do with convicts besides returning them to the
streets with scant supervision or subjecting them to the brutali-
ties of prison.

In addition, they make it possible to provide sanctions of
some meaning—community service, work for restitution—for
offenders picked up on "quality of life" charges like drinking in
public, low level drug possession or petty theft. To that extent
they add weight to a strategy of attacking minor crimes in order
to control major ones. Overall, probation based programs make
it possible to engage offenders closer to the top of the funnel, at
an early point in their criminal careers.

Doing that spares society more of their criminal behavior—by
a sizable factor—than a system that only gets serious by sending
them to prison after they have become more serious criminals.
Suppose a 17-year-old drug addict commits five burglaries per
year. If subjected to the common routine of arrest and ineffective
probation supervision, he might continue committing his burglaries for, say, three years, until the court finally sends him to
prison. When he comes out a couple of years later, his chances
for legitimate employment more blighted than ever, he is likely
to resume burglary for several more years, unless arrested again,
until he finally "ages out" of his criminality sometime in his late
twenties or early thirties. If such a 17-year-old were sent instead
to a six-month residential drug treatment program, he could
well be diverted from committing any more crimes for the rest of
his life.

Of course, he could also flunk out of treatment; without better proof of their effectiveness, isn't it premature to give such
programs an important place in the criminal justice process?
Not necessarily. Treatment managers point out that an offender
may have to return for more than one attempt, voluntarily or

under coercion, before the process "takes." That alters the calculations of effectiveness.

Consider, for example, a six-month residential program with a "success" rate—defined as the number of participants who are helped into permanent recovery from addiction—of only 20 percent. At the beginning of the first year, 100 people are arrested and sentenced to six months in the program. After six months, 20 are permanently removed from lives of drugs and crime, while 80 go back to their old ways on the streets. Assume that within the next six months, these eighty are either arrested and sentenced to another six months of treatment or can be persuaded to enroll for it voluntarily. After another six months in the program, 16 of them will be rescued from addiction and criminality, while 64 will return to the streets. Now assume that the 64 are brought into treatment once more within another six months. This time, 13 more are saved, for a total of 49.

Over two and a half years, the supposedly ineffectual program has actually rehabilitated nearly half of the criminal addicts, preventing any more criminal behavior by them for the rest of their lives. And it has incapacitated all of the addicts for 18 of the 36 months. Sending them to prison for the same period of time would prevent all the addicts from committing crimes for all of the 36 months, but it would return the vast majority of them to the streets to resume full blown criminal careers. There is no question that the community is better off sending the 100 for repeated attempts at the treatment program rather than sending them off to prison.

These calculations suggest that a massive expansion of drug treatment and other intermediate sanctions could bring rehabilitation into the criminal justice process in a big way, where it would make the most sense and do the most good in terms of crime prevention. The programs now operating also indicate a second benefit, not to be overlooked: Community service or restitution programs based on private sector employment keep offenders in touch with the law abiding public in positive ways, while removing them to prisons encourages the public to think of them in dehumanized, if not demonic terms.

Neighbors who watch a community service work crew refurbishing a playground or cleaning up the local beach after a storm find it harder to think of the offenders as malignant agents of fear. Employers who give work to "restitutioners" treat them as other employees, rewarding hard work and taking advantage of special skills. Some have even offered restitution workers permanent jobs, then promoted them to positions of responsibility. When talk turns to crime at the Rotary Club lunch, they are well positioned to point out the benefits of work that turns burglars and drug dealers into wage earners and taxpayers. The whole process keeps the crime problem in perspective and lightens up the emotion that overwhelms considered responses.

But what of those who remain impervious to the programs—the 51 left over after drug treatment has helped the fortunate 49? Despite their incorrigibility, the attempts to rehabilitate them remain important. Think again of my friend Mal. No, several experiences with intermediate sanctions were not enough to turn him around. He did have to do that himself, and he had to do it in prison. But he was willing to credit the judge nonetheless, "because he showed me how much he cared."

That suggests the ultimate reason for holding onto the rehabilitative ideal, and it is profoundly moral. America's founding fathers may have been naive about the possibility of rehabilitating people in prison, but they were not naive about the importance of rehabilitation. An ethical society can choose to use criminal justice for more than maintaining domestic peace and reinforcing values codified in law. It may also, in the spirit of John Augustus, use criminal justice to acknowledge a belief that good lurks in the hearts of people who act bad; that even the worst-seeming criminals have the capacity, in time and with help, to change for the better.

The process is as imperfect and unpredictable as humanity itself: some are helped by programs; some find salvation on their own, and some never find it at all. But it is unenlightened in the extreme to deny the capacity for change or prohibit the chance to exercise it.

That seems like a radical idea for an America that has lately resumed imposing the death penalty with some enthusiasm, and that rushed to make "three-strikes" mandatory life sentences the law of the land. But rehabilitation became radical only as the fearfulness that spread to the middle class during the 1970's and 80's caused a regression to a more primitive justice fixated on punishment, at the low end of the funnel.

Reducing crime and the fear it generates does indeed remain a better goal for policy than allowing the fear a free rein to shape justice. And crime trends in the 1990's suggest that reducing crime is possible as attention shifts to the top of the funnel. Probation-based sanctions that combine effective supervision with treatment, counseling, work and restitution are useful vehicles for pursuing that goal. As important, they send a powerful positive message about a society's deepest values, to criminals and to everyone else.

•   •   •

This book is the result of more than a year spent studying and touring the world of probation-based supervision and rehabilitation programs. It offers a snapshot of how they operated during 1995—many of them in surprisingly robust condition, given a political climate that continued to reward politicians who championed the death penalty, chain gangs, mandatory life terms for recidivists and public stigmatization of sex offenders.

To examine such programs is to be struck by the degree to which they reflect different approaches to the same problem: What to do with people arrested for behavior that, while often nonviolent, still violates the law seriously enough to incur a sentence to county jail or state prison. The surprise, given the level of public outrage over criminal violence, is the number of incarcerated convicts who fit this description. The most recent survey of state prisons, published in 1993, found that 32 percent of their inmates had been convicted of nonviolent offenses.

Many are the all too familiar cases of young people, still in adolescence or barely out of it, whose criminality plainly arises from youthful poor judgment in the face of limited options for the future. Huge numbers land in jail or prison as the result of a lifestyle based on drug or alcohol abuse. In urban lockups, more than 60 percent of people arrested for drug crimes, burglary, robbery, and larceny test positively for drugs, and about 30 percent of people sent to state prison each year are convicted of drug offenses. The substance abuse issue is often so obvious that prosecutor, judge, and defense attorney would readily agree to treatment instead of prison if treatment were available. As drug abuse grew in the late 1980s, police responded with "buy and bust" operations, loading prisons with people who had done nothing more violent than get caught in possession of a certain quantity of drugs, or selling drugs to an undercover police officer. Between 1980 and 1990, the number of people sent to state prisons each year for drug offenses more than tripled from less than 10 percent to 30 percent.

The "technical violators" of probation or parole contribute another 30 percent to the prison population. Such people are locked up not because they have committed new crimes of violence, but because they stayed out too late, got drunk, failed a drug test, or otherwise violated rules set as conditions for their supervised release from a prison sentence for an earlier crime.

All criminal offenses certainly deserve a response. But why should it invariably be the penitentiaries that inflict so relentless a burden on taxpayers, turn lightweight offenders into more dangerous criminals, and do nothing to help them confront their basic problems? The politics of fear appears to have obscured a central principle: reserve the most serious confinement and punishment for the most serious criminals. Tough sentencing laws intended to curb major violence inevitably sweep into prison tens of thousands convicted of less menacing crimes or those that involve no violence at all.

As prison expansion falls short of the demand for space, the need to accommodate all the small-time drug dealers and property offenders serving their mandatory terms makes it harder to put away the vicious rapist for life. Relieving the prisons of those who pose no threat to society and who plainly need help as well as punishment could liberate enough "hard" beds to accommodate genuinely violent convicts for years to come.

Alternative sanctions are for the most part devised and managed by state or county governments, sometimes in partnership with nonprofit organizations. While similar in concept, the details of practice and nomenclature vary widely.

Intensive probation supervision subjects some offenders to house arrest, requiring them to be at home when not at work or the probation office. Elsewhere house arrest might be part of a day-reporting program separate from intensive probation supervision. A boot camp enrolls convicted drug abusers in a therapeutic community as part of a larger regime of military drill, physical conditioning, work and counseling. A court-based diversion program requires enrollment in a stand-alone residential therapeutic community in lieu of criminal prosecution.

How then to classify programs and select a manageable few for detailed examination? Those chosen for this book show real promise either at the demonstration level or on a large scale. They succeed, for the most part, as genuine, safe alternatives to jail or prison, and they make some attempt to change criminal convicts for the better or otherwise engage them constructively—in society's terms as well as their own.

The chapters are organized to present the programs in ascending order according to severity. The first deals with community service imposed as a stand-alone sanction rather than as one element of a complex sentence. The second examines intensive supervision and house arrest regimes that allow offenders to live at home and go to work while subjecting them to strict limits and scrutiny. The third chapter describes day- reporting centers, which impose similar limits but also require daily attendance and counseling at a program office.

The fourth and fifth chapters discuss court ordered treatment for drug addicts and sex offenders, regimes that strictly limit clients' freedom and require active participation in a demanding therapy process. Residential restitution programs, described in the sixth chapter, require offenders to live in a secure setting when not working for money to repay victims. Boot camps, finally, subject offenders to physical, mental, and emotional challenges designed to teach self-discipline and otherwise prepare offenders for productive lives.

Most are "front end" programs imposed as conditions of probation; once convicted and sentenced to them, the offender never goes to jail or prison. Day reporting centers and sex offender treatment, however, may also be used as "back end" programs designed as ways to release convicts from jail or prison before they have served their full terms.

Programs for sex offenders are also anomalous as they sanction violent crimes rather than drug offenses, burglary, or theft. The offenders often begin treatment while still incarcerated, earning early release only when they show progress. Then they submit to a regime of close supervision and continued intensive therapy on an outpatient basis. Judges and corrections officials agree that a sentence including a well-managed therapy program does much more to protect public safety than a longer spell in prison followed by release with no attempt at treatment. In the bargain, of course, the programs also yield significant savings on correctional costs.

Taken as a whole, the chapters demonstrate the possibilities for a "ladder" of sanctions—a well-coordinated menu of programs that allows judges to tailor sentences for particular offenders and their offenses, and to advance offenders through increasing levels of supervision and control as needed. The penultimate chapter examines the Phoenix, Arizona, probation department's impressive attempts to do just that, demonstrating that the potential for synergy is real.

Community Service
A Productive Way to Punish

HOMELESS AT the age of 46, Martin "boosts" goods from New York City department stores, resells them for money to purchase a week or two at a cheap hotel, then steals again when the money runs out. This way of life often lands him in court, where he faces the standard sentences of sixty or ninety days in jail. Some judges, however, consider that a waste: Cells cost money, and Martin isn't that dangerous. They would rather use the leverage his conviction has given them to get some honest work out of him, and the city's Community Service Sentencing Project gives them a reliable way to do so.

That suits Martin just fine. "Jail is overcrowded," he complains. "And you have a lot of gangs going on in jail now. . . . People get stabbed up, killed." But many other New Yorkers also see the benefit of his alternative sentencing: He has cleared lots for communal gardens, cleaned up a YMCA, painted low-income housing units, and performed other sundry tasks for neighborhood groups around the city. As he and hundreds of other petty criminals do such jobs under supervision of the courts, they demonstrate both the possibilities for saving on jail costs and constructive use of work as a sanction.

Courts have ordered convicts to work in communities for hundreds of years; under ancient legal systems based on restitution, criminals labored to compensate their particular victims for injury or loss. The Romans used criminals as laborers for public works, like road construction, or as galley slaves. In the seventeenth century, offenders in England could be impressed into the navy or indentured to settlers heading out to the colonies.

The Thirteenth Amendment to the United States Constitution bans slavery and involuntary servitude but exempts work "as punishment for crime whereof the party shall have been duly convicted." For most of United States history, however, courts made little use of forced labor as a criminal sentence.

The modern era of community service sentencing began in 1966 in Alameda County, California. Judges there began imposing work assignments as an alternative to jail for indigent offenders who could not pay traffic fines. Eventually they extended use of the sanction to other low-level convicts as well.

The practice spread across the country in the late 1970s, as the federal Law Enforcement Assistance Administration (LEAA) pumped out funding to encourage it. Sentencing offenders to unpaid labor inspired some judges' creativity as they combined community service with jail or a fine or both. Offenders did low-level maintenance work for public agencies—clearing litter from playgrounds, sweeping up around public buildings or housing projects, cutting grass and raking leaves in parks, washing cars in an agency motor pool. Others did clerical work or answered phones. Thousands more were sent off to help out at hospitals, nursing homes, social service centers, and other nonprofit organizations.

There were fewer problems with unions than some predicted. Offenders in community service were doing jobs no one else would do, or jobs for which no funds were in place, so they posed no threat to union workers.

Many of these programs withered in the 1980s after the LEAA well dried up. But the concept was established. Judges appreciated the new option—more punitive than traditional probation, less punitive and more productive than incarceration. Community service sentencing provided free labor for public works or nonprofit groups, held offenders accountable for the damage they caused, and perhaps even left them with some new job or life skills to help keep them out of further trouble.

Where no special agencies existed to keep track of people sentenced to community service, probation departments took over. But with no federal program in place to monitor the practice or set standards, wide disparity characterized the imposition of community service sentences and raised troubling questions about its fairness. Debates continued over whether judges gave white middle-class offenders community service sentences for crimes that routinely landed the poor black or Hispanic criminal in prison.

Scholars like Norval Morris and Michael Tonry, in *Between Prison and Probation* (1990), could theorize about the capacity of community service to afford precision—a judge might measure a sentence to fit the seriousness of a crime in increments of days or even hours. Yet perceptions of how to do so varied widely from place to place as judges, program executives, and criminal-justice bureaucrats debated how punishment for crime ought to equate with work. In New Jersey a recidivist drunk driver might get 90 days of community service; in California the same crime drew only 90 hours.

Larger urban states continued to make extensive use of community service sentencing through the 1980s and 1990s. "Judges like it; it's relatively cheap," observes Alan Harland, a professor of criminology at Temple University who has studied community service sentencing nationwide. In recent years state legislatures have even mandated community service as part of the sentence for certain offenses. "It's seen as punitive and rehabilitative at the same time," says Sandy Seely, former head of the National Community Sentencing Association.

Thus in New Jersey, on any given day, some 40,000 people are under an order of community service. In Harris County, Texas, which surrounds Houston, 5,500 defendants perform community service each month. In the populous counties surrounding Los Angeles and San Francisco, California, judges impose the sentence on thousands of offenders per week. And even in a more rural state like North Carolina, more than 20,000 offenders are performing sentences of community service at any one time.

Judges typically impose the sentences according to formula— for example, six hours of work equal one day of jail. The offenders are interviewed to determine their skills and availability, then matched with jobs at government or nonprofit agencies. The probation department handles enforcement and eventual referral of failed cases back to the court for resentencing.

Rates of completion vary from place to place, depending on how well the programs are managed and how effectively probation departments or other law enforcement agents actually go after absentees. In New Jersey, Bill Burrell, the state's chief of Adult Probation Services and Community Service, claims a completion rate of 85 percent for his large community service work force, while in Indiana the programs run by Prisoners and Community Together (PACT) show completion rates of about 80 percent. PACT assigns caseworkers to work full time on supervision of offenders, visiting the work sites and documenting their progress. In other places, however, supervision and follow-up are much more haphazard; all too often a court learns that offenders failed to complete community service orders only when they are arrested for new crimes.

It is hard to determine how much community service serves as a substitute for jail or prison. The argument for the sanction looks compelling: Sentencing a person to community service spares the huge expense of incarceration. Yet during the 1970s and early 1980s, researchers seeking out genuine cases of convicts doing community service instead of time behind bars came up relatively empty handed.

In a 1982 article for *Corrections Magazine*, Kevin Krajick found a few places where community service appeared to have prevented incarceration of juveniles and only two that credibly did so for adults. These were the Community Service Sentencing Project started in New York City by the Vera Institute of Justice and the Indiana-based Prisoners and Community Together program. PACT, Krajick reported, set a policy of accepting only convicted felons or misdemeanants who had pleaded down from felony charges. Program officials estimated that without the community service option, about half of the offenders in the program would have gone to jail or prison.

There is some reason to believe that use of the sanction as a genuine alternative increased in subsequent years. As courts continued to feel the pressures of jail crowding, the advantages of community service appeared more obvious than ever, and judges sought ways to make the most of it. As the federal government brought pressure for tougher laws against drunk driving, for example, community service became the sentence of choice, especially for offenders with stable jobs and families. Seely says that today, even drunk drivers found guilty of vehicular homicide may wind up working off their debt to society at a community service site rather then doing time behind bars. "It's a sentence that the victim's family usually agrees to," she says.

In addition, states that impose escalating sanctions—intensive probation supervision, electronic monitoring, day treatment, restitution—that substitute for jail may include community service as part of a sentence package. And a few jurisdictions have set up programs that substitute community service for jail but call it something else.

California, for example, runs a sizable "work release" program for people who otherwise would be serving jail terms of a few days or a week. Offenders sentenced to the custody of the county sheriff may qualify if they have roots in the community, family ties, and a nonviolent record. Elsewhere work release means allowing inmates to work at paying jobs on the outside as they approach the end of jail or prison confinement. But California's work release offenders never see the inside of a county jail. Instead they report for work cleaning beaches and parks, painting public buildings, or doing other work under constant supervision of a deputy sheriff. In most places that would be called a community service sentence.

New York's Community Service Sentencing Project (CSSP), funded by contracts with New York City and New York State, manages a caseload of 50 to 60 offenders on any given day, for a total of 1,800 per year. It began operations in 1979 as an experiment of the Vera Institute of Justice, a nonprofit group known for its innovations and research on urban problems, but now operates as part of a freestanding agency.

The CSSP's long record of sound management gives it formidable credibility with the courts and a good reputation with politicians and the news media. CSSP offenders perform some 90,000 hours of community work per year; recidivism rates are no higher than for offenders sent to jail. More than 70 percent of offenders sentenced to CSSP successfully complete their work assignments. About 75 percent of those who fail, go back before the courts; overall nearly 90 percent of offenders sentenced to the program either do the work or go to jail.

That level of completion satisfies the courts. "It's regarded highly by the judges," says Justice Charles Solomon, supervising judge of the Manhattan Criminal Court. "It's more meaningful to have someone do two weeks of real work than to sit in a jail cell for two weeks." He reiterates that the program has "a lot of credibility. If someone doesn't do it, we'll know. We'll see them back again."

By now the CSSP's representatives are familiar figures in city courtrooms. Their job is to screen defendants as they come into court and participate in plea negotiations with prosecutors and defense attorneys. Defendants with violent records are eliminated, as are those with more than 50 prior arrests. But so are those with no priors at all, on the assumption that they would not be sentenced to jail in any event. The defendants also must submit to an interview with court representatives who insist that they have a verifiable home address and otherwise tell the truth.

Those who survive the grilling gain a strong advocate. The court representative goes before the judge and prosecutor to argue for community service, emphasizing the offender's ties to the community, the need to hold down jail crowding, and the benefits a neighborhood will reap from the offender's work.

Once sentenced, the offenders are told to report to CSSP locations in the basements of housing projects. The work day starts with coffee and doughnuts, followed by a bit of leaf raking, snow removal, or trash pickup to compensate the project for use of its space. The supervisors take attendance and dispatch members of the CSSP enforcement team—set up in the late 1980s to shore up completion rates— to go after the no-shows. The enforcers make two or three attempts to find recalcitrants or roust them out of bed. After that they go to court for arrest warrants.

Meanwhile vans take the rest of the group to the day's main work sites. Unlike many other community service programs, CSSP offenders work only for small non-profit organizations. A typical day might find them digging soil and hauling gravel to prepare a community garden, clearing construction debris at a parochial school, or painting the halls of a nursing home. From the beginning the project rejected work for city and state agencies. There were potential conflicts with civil service unions and the work requirements were less flexible.

"With the nonprofits, we can call up and say we have a crew ready to come over now," explains Joel Copperman, the program's executive director. "Try saying that to a government agency." Besides, he adds, work for the neighborhood groups "seems to be the most valued. It's been our way of giving back to the community in the most direct way."

Developing the worksites became a full time job for Clayton Williams, an ex-convict who found employment at Vera and became a member of the staff that first implemented CSSP. He roamed the neighborhoods of New York City looking for promising patches of urban decay: a vacant lot in need of greening, a dilapidated building intended to house the homeless mentally ill, a parochial school's leaf-strewn play yard.

His efforts and the work of the CSSP offenders don't go unappreciated. "They come out and do everything," says Idonia Johnson, a neighborhood leader who called on CSSP when she and her neighbors needed help with heavy digging to turn an empty lot into a garden. "Planting, cleaning, doing the beds. They're very nice to work with. We never had any problem with them." (Indeed, for a time Ms. Johnson felt so grateful that she prepared sumptuous chicken dishes to bring over for lunch, causing some competition among the offenders for assignment to her site.)

The crews work under the constant supervision of CSSP staff membersrecruited for their street smarts and their ability to handle occasional arguments, bouts of recalcitrance, or pleas for time off to take care of urgent business. A standard response to the person with a problem at the welfare office or a sick relative: How would you handle it if you were in jail? At the beginning and at the end of the shift, however, offenders have a chance to meet with caseworkers who assess needs and try to solve problems that might get in the way of reporting for work. An offender who shows up on a cold day without warm clothes may get boots and a coat. Homeless offenders get money for flophouse rooms; some also get help with food, child care, and referrals for medical care or substance abuse treatment.

Despite the occasional hassles offenders are unanimous in saying they'd much rather be working for the program than doing time in a city jail. Some say the community service sentence, modest an interruption as it might be in the context of their whole lives, has some rehabilitative effect. CSSP is "showing me how to be a more responsible person, as far as getting up on time for work and what have you," says Jerry. "I know that there's an eight month sentence hanging over my head [should he fail to complete the 70 hours], so I get up."

The only substantive complaint offenders voice arises from their disappointment at the loss of help with food, clothes, and housing expenses after they complete their community service obligation. They also lament that after the program gives them a healthy taste of honest work, they have to give it up.

"When it's over with, you're on your own again," Martin says. "You're back to day one again. You leave. Where do you go?" He believes the program ought to offer services "that can gear you to staying out here, so you don't have to do those things you do" to survive on the streets.

Richard, serving his third community service sentence, concurs. "I think this would be a better program if it was geared more towards setting people up with actual jobs . . . you leave here and what are you going to do? You go back and do the same things you did before to get money."

CSSP managers express some skepticism that the motivation to work would continue for many of the offenders if a work-placement component were added. For now, in any case, says Copperman, "It's not what we do. We're not an employment program. We're punishment."

In the beginning, New York City officials and Vera's planners saw the Community Service Sentencing Project as a way both to ease pressure on crowded jails and to establish a tougher sanction for low-level offenders who got off with light probation supervision or had charges dismissed. Funders and corrections policy experts objected that community service sentences for the second group would "widen the net" of social control. But in a memo on the subject a Vera executive held out for their inclusion, arguing that "the net of social control is presently inadequate." In the end they agreed to divide the caseload half and half between those bound for jail and those likely to receive fines or simple probation. A second decision concerned sentence length. All offenders sentenced to community service, the Vera planners decided, would do the same seventy hours of work. This denied judges the chance to fine-tune sentences to fit crimes, one of the basic theoretical selling points of community service. But Vera officials were determined that sentences would be completed, and they worried that they might not be able to coax or compel people to work for more than two weeks.

Similar pragmatism guided a third decision: to offer community service only as punishment, with no broader claims of rehabilitation. If they bought that idea, courts and the public would more easily accept the sanction as a substitute for jail. Besides, it seemed disingenuous to describe forced, menial, unpaid labor any other way.

In another choice with long-term implications, the Vera managers also decided to administer community service from a freestanding agency rather than turning it over to the probation department, as was widely done elsewhere. The separate agency, they hoped, would preserve the identity of community service as a punishment in its own right and as a real substitute for jail.

The program's managers still like to tell the story of its first client, a young man named Willie, who provided an immediate test of the planner's assumptions. Convicted of stealing a $20 pair of trousers from a department store, Willie had seemed like a sound candidate. But he failed to show up for his first day of work. The staff panicked: After all the careful preparation, would the project fail with its first case?

Willie had given a number of addresses and could not be found at any of them. But his screening papers also noted that he was enrolled in a methadone maintenance program. Clayton Williams, then a work supervisor, looked it up and went over the next morning. "They may not go to school, they may not go to work, they may not even go home," he remembers thinking, "but they're going to this methadone program" because the alternative was the illness of withdrawal. Williams explained who he was, and the benefits of the new program, to all who would listen at the clinic. When Willie finally walked in at the end of the day, Williams recalls, "Everybody jumped on him, the director, . . . the case managers, his friends"—all berating him for not taking advantage of the community service sentence.

Willie reported faithfully to work for the next two weeks, and community service sentencing was finally up and running.

That year Bronx judges sent 5 to 7 offenders per month to the project. Most completed the sentence without problems. The following year the numbers increased. By the end of 1980 more than 300 offenders had participated, and Vera moved to expand the program with offices in other boroughs of the city.

Though the level of acceptance continued to increase, program administrators found themselves fighting hard at a couple of points during the 1980s to sustain its credibility. The first challenge concerned the number of jail-bound cases. An analysis of cases between October 1, 1981, and September 30, 1982, showed that citywide about 45 percent of convicts doing community service would otherwise have gone to jail—close to the fifty-fifty split planners had set as a goal. But there were big differences among the boroughs. The figure for Manhattan was more than 60 percent, while the figure for Brooklyn was an unacceptable 28 percent and the figure for the Bronx was an even lower 20 percent.

In 1983 a new director, Judy Greene, took over the program determined to increase the Brooklyn and Bronx figures for jail-bound offenders. Percentages were low in those boroughs, she found, because prosecutors had gained too much influence over selection of cases for the project. She required that cases be taken from court dockets rather than prosecutors' files, and she denied prosecutors the chance to veto selected candidates. These changes quickly increased the percentages of jail diversions to 52 percent in the Bronx and 57 percent in Brooklyn.

Problems with enforcement caused another crisis a few years later. From Clayton Williams's first-day pursuit of Willie, Vera had been determined to make the offenders do the work; especially given the relatively short seventy-hour sentence, the program's managers believed a high rate of completion was essential to preserving the court's belief in community service as a viable substitute for jail.

If supervisors weren't able to locate absent offenders and persuade them to return to work, they sent warning letters, then notified either the prosecutor or the judge of the default. The court would issue summonses, followed by arrest warrants for those who failed to appear. Judges were stern with absconders, giving jail terms of six months or more to replace the two weeks of community service.

This process produced impressive success rates in the early years; Douglas McDonald, who examined the program in *Punishment Without Walls* (1986), reports that through June 1983, 86 percent of the Bronx offenders had completed their sentences. For Brooklyn and Manhattan, the figures were 85 percent and 89 percent.

By 1986, however, the spread of crack and other intensifying social problems stressed the community service program along with the rest of criminal justice. The completion rate plummeted. The project's managers tried to respond by sending out new "compliance agents" to find and confront the no-shows and by hiring "participant monitors" to help individual offenders with the problems that were preventing them from getting to work. But the social work approach wasn't enough to stem the absenteeism. Returning cases to the courts, meanwhile, had little immediate effect, since the city police units responsible for enforcing arrest warrants had become overwhelmed. An offender would face consequences for failure to complete community service only if the fact came to light after an arrest for a new offense.

By 1987 the completion rate had slumped to 50 percent, and the program faced a potentially disastrous erosion of credibility. Another new director, Susan Powers, decided on a drastic response: She set up her own armed enforcement unit to go after truants so that she would not have to rely on city police. This was possible under a law authorizing the designation of "special patrolmen" for such a purpose but required several months of negotiation with the police department. In the end the department gave its blessing, and Powers fielded a team recruited from the ranks of retired police officers. The plan worked. The new unit halted the slide in completions; within a few years the rate had climbed back to a healthier 70 percent.

If strong management has kept the program on track, however, it cannot provide answers to more fundamental questions. One concerns public safety. Offenders sentenced to CSSP are under supervision of the program for only ten days when they might have served jail sentences of one or two months. Because many are chronic recidivists who would have been incapacitated longer in jail, additional crime may well be another cost of community service. In his study of the Vera project, McDonald calculated the rate of additional offenses at fifteen arrests per 100 people sentenced to the program.

Copperman responds that the point is now "all so speculative," since it is based on ten-year-old research that has not been updated. CSSP graduates have yet to generate scandalous headlines with horrible crimes that might have been prevented had they gone to jail. And Justice Solomon considers it an issue of slight concern. He emphasizes that offenders sentenced to community service are screened to eliminate any with histories of violence. There might be a small risk of more nonviolent crimes, but to the extent community service manages to keep people out of jail, it makes possible the incarceration of more dangerous criminals. "That's the philosophy," he asserts. CSSP "is really designed to free up jail space for more violent offenders."

The problem might be remedied, of course, by abandoning the uniform seventy-hour sentence and requiring community service for periods that approximate possible jail terms. But Copperman hesitates to embrace the idea. Longer sentences would require more staff the program can't afford. And there is no certainty the success rate could be sustained even with more staff. "If you're going to create a program with enormous failure rates, then you're never going to get anywhere," Copperman argues.

Another difficult question concerns costs. What is the dollar value of cells the program saves or frees for use by more violent offenders? CSSP operates on an annual budget of $2.9 million in funding from New York City and New York State. By the most optimistic estimates, the 1800 clients sentenced to the program for two-week terms would otherwise occupy the equivalent of 250 jail beds per year. Since the annual cost of one bed is $58,400, it's tempting to claim a saving in jail costs of $14.6 million per year, for a net saving to taxpayers of $11.7 million.

Yet it's misleading to calculate the total saving that way, since those 250 beds remain so tiny a fraction of the city jail system's 20,000 bed capacity. As McDonald points out, no cellblocks are closed down, no guards are laid off for the sake of so small a reduction in bed use. The real saving amounts only to the marginal cost of a prisoner's daily care—food, toiletries and the like— certainly no more than, by generous estimate, $20 per bed per day, or $7,300 per year. On that basis the saving totals only $1.8 million for the 250 beds, and community service sentencing, with a total operating expense of $2.9 million, actually costs the taxpayers $1.1 million per year. The program also generates the value of the work done for the nonprofit groups—about $450,000 a year if one values the 90,000 hours at $5 per hour. But none of that affects the city budget.

Copperman doesn't contest the point. "We recognize," he says, "that if we can't save 750 bed years [enough to begin making some jail staff and plant reductions possible] then we're probably not saving anything, because the fixed costs are enormous."

Even so, the fact that the city has not chosen to take full advantage of it hardly negates the program's potential. New York's experience still demonstrates that given tough, thoughtful management, community service can ease pressure on jails while making offenders accountable for crimes in a way the public will support.

Intensive Supervision, Probation, and House Arrest
Saving Money on the System

SPRING BRINGS on the serious heat and humidity in Tampa—
shorts weather for sure—and that creates a special problem for
certain state probation clients. Elizabeth copes by mastering her
anger, Tim relies on old fashioned honesty, while Ellen uses a scarf.

Their problem: the conspicuously ugly electronic monitoring
device each wears strapped to an ankle. When Elizabeth, convicted of a drug charge, goes out in warm weather, people say,
"'You got a beeper on your leg! Look at her; she's got a box on
her leg!'" she laments. "I get angry . . . . I get real mad at them.
But I ignore that. It's something I've got to do."

"I'll wear shorts," says Tim, a twenty-year-old who stole a
car. "I don't care. If people ask, I tell them what it is. I did [the
crime], so I'm not going to lie about it."

Ellen, who shoplifted to support her cocaine habit, rarely gets
asked. The colorful bandanna she ties around her ankle effectively disguises the black box and its strap. "Very few people

look at your ankles anyway, observes the bar hostess who spent most of her younger days working as a topless dancer.

The three are participating in the most restrictive form of a probation-based house arrest program established in 1983 to ease pressure on Florida's chronically crowded prisons. On a given day, more than 14,000 Floridians are subject to the special scrutiny of probation officers with small caseloads and a penchant for frequent drug tests and surprise visits; about 1,000 clients bear the additional constraint of electronic surveillance around the clock.

The program has clearly solved a problem for Florida; it is used routinely by the courts and has been incorporated into sentence guidelines. Corrections officials, judges, and state legislators agree that it succeeds as an effective tool of prison-population management.

Florida's house arrest program developed from the national trend toward "intensive supervision probation" (also called intensive probation supervision—ISP and IPS) that took hold in the 1980s. The Georgia Department of Corrections was one of the first to give officers small caseloads and the time and resources required to devote heightened attention to their cases. The idea was to permit serious enforcement of probation conditions and restore probation's credibility as a sanction. The agency's own early evaluations portrayed intensive supervision as highly cost effective. Recidivism rates were low; clients went to work and contributed part of their earnings for restitution to victims and fees to make the program self-supporting. The state's corrections director claimed that intensive supervision had averted construction of two new prisons. By the end of the decade all fifty states had implemented intensive supervision probation, many according to the Georgia model.

The typical program reduced probation officers' caseloads to between 25 and 50, from 100 or more, and required offenders to meet with officers at least a few times per week, sometimes even daily, rather than a few times per month. The clients might be summoned for urinalysis drug testing at any time and could expect rigid enforcement of curfews and other limits. They might also be required to participate in counseling programs, come up with regular payments for fines, court costs, and restitution, and perform community service. States saw intensive probation as a genuine alternative to incarceration for nonviolent offenders, a new sanction halfway between prison and traditional probation.

While the appeal was enough to establish the practice nation-wide, the early optimism faded as problems arose. In some places, judges and prosecutors refused to divert prison-bound offenders to intensive probation, using it only as one option among others for low-level cases. And the intensive programs began to show high failure rates as offenders who were held to tight standards wound up in violation of the rules. Diversion benefits of intensive supervision melted away as judges sent the technical violators to prison.

A 1990 General Accounting Office (GAO) report on intensive supervision probation reinforced the doubts. It pointed out that most ISP programs were too small to generate cost savings from prison diversion. Taking several dozen or even a few hundred inmates out of a prison system housing tens of thousands did not result in big staff reductions or cellblock closings. Moving those inmates into ISP required substantial new hiring of probation officers. Meanwhile, the GAO noted, revocations of ISP cases would result in new incarceration costs. The net result could be an increase in correctional spending as a direct result of ISP.

Other researchers questioned the assumption that intensive supervision actually controlled crime more than regular probation supervision. Early research suggesting that it did, they argued, did not control for offender mix—ISP might be showing good recidivism statistics simply because more benign offenders were being assigned to it. A 1986 study funded by the Bureau of

Justice Assistance (BJA) controlled for offender mix at 14 sites in nine states. It found no real diversions or cost savings, and offenders on ISP committed new crimes at the same rates as those on conventional probation or parole.

Joan Petersilia and Susan Turner, two researchers for the RAND Corporation who spent several years involved in the BJA study, did find two positive results. First, there appeared to be no correlation between technical violations and new criminal offenses. This finding countered conventional wisdom holding that once a client begins to violate conditions of probation, new crimes cannot be far behind. Petersilia and Turner suggested that since this apparently is not the case, ISP administrators should consider limits on technical violations and punishments for them as a way to save money.

Second, in the California ISP programs Petersilia and Turner studied directly, they found lower rates of recidivism for offenders involved in substance abuse treatment and other social service programs than for those who were not. A management policy that stints on resources for such services in favor of surveillance, they suggested, could be self-defeating.

Other inquiries found more encouraging results in individual states. A GAO study published in 1993, for example, examined intensive supervision probation as implemented in Maricopa and Pima counties in Arizona. It found lower numbers of intensive supervision clients arrested for new crimes than those on standard probation, though when the intensive clients moved over to standard probation, as most did, they began committing new crimes at a higher rate.

The researchers also examined histories of comparable offenders who spent time in prison followed by time on parole. While the Maricopa County offenders committed no new crimes in prison, their rate of new crimes on parole was so high that after three years almost as many had been arrested as had those on IPS followed by standard probation.

The researchers found that the costs of intensive supervision cases were generally lower than those of the prison cases, even including costs of revocation and return to prison. In Maricopa County, for example, each intensive supervision case cost $3,941 less than a similar case sent to prison followed by parole for the most serious crimes; for each less serious case the saving was $1,621; the least serious cases resulted in a slight cost increase of $350 over prison because prison terms for such offenses were so much shorter than sentences to intensive supervision.

During the 1980s, many probation departments turned to a form of intensive supervision known as home confinement or house arrest. Offenders were required to remain in their homes if not at work, the probation office, a therapy group, or another activity approved in advance. Joan Petersilia estimated that by 1987 between 10,000 and 20,000 offenders were subject to house arrest nationwide on any given day.

Probation officers enforced house arrest with frequent, random visits, or phone calls. But the effectiveness of such supervision was doubtful. Offenders simply waited for an officer's evening visit and then went out assuming that the officer would not be back that night. An officer could try to thwart such violations by doubling back for a quick second visit. But that wasn't possible every night for every client, even with a small caseload.

Technology provided an answer in the form of electronic monitors that subject offenders to more reliable scrutiny around the clock. Experiments with such devices date back to the 1960s, but their use swelled during the late 1980s with the general expansion of house arrest. Marc Renzema, a student of the practice, estimated that by 1990 there were 12,000 offenders subject to electronic monitoring in forty-seven states, up from only 95 offenders in seven states four years before.

By then the industry had settled on two approaches. Programmed contact supervision relies on a telephone robot to call offenders homes at random; the offender must verify his or her presence either by voice or by placing a wristlet in a special receptacle attached to the phone. The more sophisticated radio frequency approach requires the offender to wear an anklet fitted with a transmitter sending constant radio signals to a receiver/dialer attached to the phone. The dialer periodically calls a central monitoring station so that a computer there can verify that transmissions from the offender's anklet are being received. Since the anklet transmitter has a range of only 100 to 150 feet, the offender may not stray too far from the phone.

Offenders supervised by both methods submit itineraries documenting their whereabouts hour by hour, noting approved absences from home for work, school, substance abuse therapy, or visits to the probation office. The itineraries are used to program monitoring computers so that they send alarm messages to the probation office only when they detect unapproved absences.

The devices appeared to offer two undeniable advantages: Most offenders found the idea of an electronic sensor controlled by a computer far more intimidating than mere human being. Unless they could get the anklets off somehow, they truly believed they couldn't leave home without getting caught. And a public growing used to computers, cellular phones, and other marvels of modern electronics responded positively to the idea and found it reassuring.

As commonly happens with the introduction of new technology, however, it took some time before reality could approach the theoretical promise. Early versions of the devices weren't reliable; handy offenders learned to cut off the anklets and leave them by the phone, then reassemble them with super glue. A person with a slender ankle could remove the device with the help of Vaseline, then slip it on the cat, who remains at home as his owner goes off to party with friends. At the monitoring station, software foul-ups set off alarms for authorized absences as well as genuine violations, causing much aggravation and wasted time. Power surges and lightning strikes could scramble the whole system. Waterbeds, cast iron bathtubs, metal-clad mobile homes, and other elements of an offender's environment also interfered with transmissions.

All this diminished the capacity of the devices to make house arrest less labor intensive. "While electronic monitoring equipment automates the basic monitoring process, it also creates a considerable amount of work," observe Terry L. Baumer and Robert I. Mendelsohn, who published a major study of electronic monitoring in 1990. "In providing more intensive monitoring, the automated process produces its own configuration of tasks and duties, which may be more time-consuming and costly than manual methods of monitoring."

Such findings, seized upon by critics who objected to the idea of a high-tech substitute for supervision based on human contact, may overstate the case against electronic monitoring. As agencies discovered bugs, the electronic monitoring industry consolidated and dealt with technical problems. And while savings on probation staff may be diminished by the need for additional work to manage an electronic system, the system itself still can serve as a powerful tool to increase the effectiveness of supervision in the community. As it does that, it can save enough on jail or prison beds—even with increased technical violations—to produce net reductions in costs.

Baumer and Mendelsohn even found an intrinsic rehabilitative aspect to the sanction. They interviewed offenders so intimidated by house arrest that it caused them to alter their conduct for the better. In interviews with the researchers, the offenders confirmed that the sanction helped them to "dry out" from alcohol abuse, renew relationships with their families, complete home improvement projects, hold on to steady jobs, and generally reexamine the course of their lives.

"In the rush to satisfy demands for punitive incarceration, the rehabilitative potential of home confinement may have been seriously underestimated," Baumer and Mendelsohn conclude.

"There is evidence that home confinement actually encourages offenders to work. In addition, the sanction appears to stabilize and structure the lives of many offenders while they are being supervised. The challenge is for programs to translate these temporary behavioral changes into more enduring personal habits."

In the meantime, entrepreneurs sensing a major market continue to work on the technology. The latest generation, just being introduced in 1997, uses global positioning satellites that communicate with anklet transceivers to track offenders wherever they go. The system generates maps that pinpoint an offender's exact location. Beyond enforcing compliance with conditions of supervised release, the system promises much in the way of crime prevention. If it works as planned, it would allow probation officers to designate certain areas—the block where a spousal abuser's wife is living; the schoolyard of interest to the compulsive pedophile—off limits and receive alarms whenever the offender enters them. The satellites would report to a central database, which probation officers could access from anywhere with a computer and a modem.

Florida amply demonstrates the positive potential for intensive supervision probation, including house arrest, when implemented on a large scale and incorporated as a staple of corrections. The emphasis is on home confinement as punishment; efforts at rehabilitation are secondary. The program fills a need: Since 1983, Florida's judges have placed more than 136,000 offenders in an intensive supervision program known as Community Control. It was conceived to serve as a genuine alternative to prison, enacted along with new sentence guidelines in 1983, and an independent study in 1990 deemed it an "unqualified success" as it reduced the state's need for prison cells without creating any new threat to public safety.

Florida's sentencing chart positions Community Control as an option between prison and regular probation or jail. Offenders given the sentence become part of caseloads that are not supposed to exceed twenty-five per probation officer. A person on Community Control must stay at home at all times except when working or attending drug treatment, school, or other approved activities.

"If Valentine's Day comes around, please don't ask and expect us to be able to let you and your girlfriend go to Red Lobster for dinner. Please don't be upset when we tell you Christmas Day that you can't go to grandma's," says Carrie Alexander, a community corrections officer. Offenders on the program are also required to pay restitution, court costs, and other fees, and may be ordered to perform community service.

Unlike treatment-oriented regimes that permit probation officers to ease restrictions for offenders who make progress, the conditions of Community Control remain fixed for the duration of the sentence or until a judge decides to change them. House arrest may continue for as long as two years, but judges often are willing to "roll over" a Community Control case to standard probation once the offender has completed a year without a violation.

In 1987 Florida's corrections department persuaded the state legislature to authorize Community Control II, which adds electronic monitoring to the basic conditions of house arrest for certain offenders. By that time more than 14,000 clients had participated in Community Control; the department believed 75 percent of them would otherwise have gone to jail or prison. The monitoring program would target technical violators of Community Control as well as offenders who could qualify for prison under the state's sentence guidelines but have no previous prison records.

The push for a serious electronic monitoring program followed a year and a half of experiments with "passive" monitoring devices like beepers and telephone robots that made periodic calls to offenders' homes. The new radio frequency program offered constant supervision twenty-four hours per day.

The offenders and Community Control officers agree on individual itineraries, then feed them to a central computer, which calls the offender's home phone every ninety seconds to check for a response. A computer that detects an unauthorized absence sends a fax to the Community Control officer and alerts a live operator who follows up with more calls.

Most of Florida's Community Control II cases are monitored with hardware provided by BI Incorporated, a Colorado-based concern that supplies the equipment for free but charges the probation division $2.49 per client per day for surveillance services, an amount defrayed in part by the $1.00 per client per day the division may collect from offenders for monitoring costs. A computer and live operators based in Indianapolis handle the Florida cases, communicating via fax and telephone.

From a pilot program of 40 monitoring units, Community Control II has grown to more than 1,000 cases, or 7 percent of the current Community Control caseload of 14,100. Operating around the clock, the electronic monitor increases the average number of surveillance "contacts" from the 79 a Community Control officer can make in person each month to more than 72,000.

There is no question that the big-brother level of supervision works. "The thing with regular house arrest is, you could go see somebody, let's say, at midnight . . . and they're going to pretty much assume that when you leave after that, you may not be coming back so they can go down and see their buddies," says Community Control officer Mark Johnson. "With this, obviously they can't do that." His colleague Michael Juliano adds that the electronic monitor "does make a big difference . . . They are constantly reminded with that anklet on that no matter when they leave. . . . we are going to be advised of it. . . . They have that constant reminder on their leg," which acts as a deterrent.

Offenders tend to agree. Tim, who did time on Community Control before his sentence to the ankle bracelet, says Community Control II "is much easier. . . . With the bracelet, you can't leave. Without the bracelet, you leave, you get caught, and you get violated. . . . They'll know if you leave with the bracelet."

"I believe that if I didn't have the monitor, I'd probably be violating," says Elizabeth. "I'd feel like I have more freedom, that he's not going to catch me, and I go and then he comes and I'm violated. I'm glad I did get this. I'm going through a drug program . . . . I graduate next month."

Even so, Florida probation officials warn against expecting too much from technology. Probation officers are required to install the units in their clients' homes, a task that requires training in the basics of telephone wiring. Where phones aren't installed properly, the probation officer may wind up reinstalling the whole phone connection. Even a simple installation may take half an hour or longer as the officer makes test calls to verify communication with the central computer in Indianapolis. David Karas, a probation supervisor, estimates that the mechanical aspects of the job alone increase the officer's workload for a Community Control II client by about 25 percent.

Furthermore, greater supervision means more offenders caught violating terms of probation, and that translates into more work for probation officers. On regular house arrest, Karas explains, "if the guy left at one o'clock in the morning and got back at two in the morning, went and got some beer or whatever, you aren't going to know about that . . . whereas our people are going to know that guy left and they're going to have to do something about it."

"Our experience has been that it hasn't decreased staff," asserts Joe Papy, a regional corrections administrator for southwest Florida. "It shouldn't be touted as being a program that . . . will pay for itself because you can cut staff." He also worries that news media and vendors eager to promote electronic monitoring tend to oversell it to a public fascinated with advancing technology. They "tend to build this picture to the public that when the machine goes off . . . there are people just rushing to the house," he laments, when the reality is likely to be a violation report that an officer brings up with the offender the following

day. "A lot of folks believe that it's a tracking system," Papy
observes, when the truth is more limited. "It doesn't tell us
where the offender is; it simply tells us where they're not."

A number of the units are also stolen each year by offenders
who abscond. Some try to sell them to friends and neighbors as
devices that enhance stereo sound or television reception. But in
one case, detectives who made an arrest found the suspect still
wearing the anklet he had been given two years before. Afraid
that taking it off might set off an alarm, he had continued to
wear it as a fugitive.

Beyond the practical issues, some Floridians raise questions
about a program that relies so fundamentally on surveillance
without building in more rehabilitative services and positive
incentives for good behavior. As a result, they say, Community
Control still suffers from the traditional ISP problems with high
revocation rates. In the fiscal year ending June 30, 1994, for
example, 16,230 offenders were put on community control and
9,533 had their status revoked because of new crimes or technical violations, for a failure rate of 59 percent. That compared
with an overall failure rate of 44 percent for all types of probation, parole, and other forms of community supervision.

Stuart Sheres, an assistant state attorney who spent many
years as a public defender, says he would try to dissuade clients
from taking the sentence in lieu of a short term in jail or prison.
"Everybody inevitably was arrested for going and picking up
cigarettes at the Seven-Eleven or walking out of the house," he
says. "The Community Control officer would go by and find
them out or someone would rat on them. . . . People just couldn't
stay at home." Community Control II, he acknowledges,
"works better, for what it's worth."

The program's defenders, however, declare that it is worth a
lot and that defense attorneys may not be in a position to appreciate the larger dynamic of the program as it works today.
Because of Community Control II, they say, not that many of the

59 percent revoked on Community Control are sent to jail or prison. Instead, a majority of the violators is simply fitted with electronic monitors and moved over to Community Control II. In one month, for example, there were 617 revocations of Community Control; of those, 137 were for new offenses and 437 were for technical violations. Most of the technical violators were put on Community Control II.

Even the doubters therefore agree that by diverting some offenders and delaying others' entrance to prison, house arrest succeeds as a way to help manage the prison population. House arrest in Florida, acknowledges Dudley Clapp of the public defender's office, "wasn't instituted because of the rehabilitative nature" but because of "pure money, hoping that it can save money on the system, and, no question, it probably does."

The only piece of objective research on the program, a 1990 study by Christopher Baird and Dennis Wagner of the National Council on Crime and Delinquency, confirms that view. The two examined the records and backgrounds of offenders on Community Control to determine how they would have been sentenced if the program did not exist. It found that 54 percent on house arrest would have gone to prison. Another 32 percent would have spent time in jail. Only 14 percent of those in the house arrest program would have been sentenced to regular probation.

"Given the rather grim record of other alternative programs," the researchers commented, "a prison diversion rate that exceeds 50 percent constitutes an unqualified success." That success, they observed, has resulted in large measure because "the Florida Community Control initiative is not an experimental program, as are most state efforts to divert offenders from prison to an intermediate sanction. Community Control is a fully articulated sentencing option in Florida that has been available for several years and is recognized in state law." The program's incorporation into the 1983 sentencing guidelines did much to insure its acceptance and serious use.

Skeptics point out that Florida's prison population has continued to climb despite the use of Community Control. But Baird and Wagner also compared a group of offenders sentenced before the guidelines with a similar group sentenced after 1983 and found that 10 percent more went to prison under the guidelines, offsetting savings on prison beds because of Community Control. "The program did not prevent Florida's prisons from becoming overcrowded," the researchers concluded, "but the crowding problem Florida is experiencing would be much worse had the Community Control Program not been implemented."

They also found that the diversion did not create any extra threat to public safety. The researchers followed offenders for 18 months after release from prison and compared their behavior with offenders followed for 18 months after beginning house arrest. The Community Control cases were rearrested at a rate of 29.4 percent, compared with a rate of 24.3 percent for those released from prison. But all of the former prisoners were arrested for new offenses, while only 19.7 percent of the Community Control cases were picked up for new crimes. The other 9.7 percent had been caught committing technical violations like leaving the house to do an errand or hang out with friends, behavior that posed no immediate danger to the public.

In addition, the researchers calculated savings to taxpayers because of diversions to jail and prison from Community Control. These were substantial: Even after deductions for the cost of reincarcerating the relatively numerous technical violators and for imposing more expensive house arrest on people who would have gotten regular probation, the state saved an average of $2,746 for every Community Control case. With admissions of more than 10,000 per year, the savings may approach or exceed $300 million annually.

The research was conducted in 1987 and 1988, just as electronic monitoring was being introduced. The number of offenders involved was still too small to support conclusions, but the researchers looked forward to Community Control II as a new sanction for technical violators of Community Control, a prospect that was borne out in fact.

The need for such a program remains clear even in a state where legislators pride themselves on toughness against crime. Their embrace of house arrest to manage crushing budget realities underscores the importance of alternative programs as a fundamental part of a state's corrections apparatus.

The lawmakers' attitude, says Community Control officer Buck Edwards, is that "in two years, you're not going to rehabilitate them. We know that—but if you keep them out of prison. . . that's less money we have to spend on them in prison."

Day Reporting
The Lessons of a Structured Life

THE GLOOMY central hall of the brick jailhouse in Springfield, Massachusetts, saw plenty of traditional justice in the years it served as the seat of law enforcement and corrections in Hampden County. Modern film directors like to hire the 108-year-old brick building for gothic scenes of crime and punishment. A trap door in the ceiling recalls a grisly bit of history: One day in 1888 a person plummeted from it to become the victim of the state's last public hanging.

These days the hall houses justice of another sort. Once a week several dozen men and a few women pull up chairs for discussions of the program that helps them put their lives back on track.

"Think about it," says Juan, gesturing to two of his friends in the group. "A couple months ago, Tommy, Frank, and I were sitting around talking about how we could help each other get out of jail and stay out of trouble. Now here we all are; we're actually doing it." Frank, Tommy, and the rest nod in hearty agreement.

People come to the old Hampden County jailhouse today to participate in what may be American correction's best example of a relatively new idea: the day reporting center. A big portion of the 150 or so enrolled in the program on a given day would otherwise be behind bars. About half are using the program to fulfill the last several months of sentences to the new Hampden county jail located in Ludlow, a few miles to the east. The rest include arrestees awaiting trial, people sentenced to probation, probation and parole violators, and a few convicts recently released from federal prisons.

All are allowed to live at home but must report to the center at least once a day in person. They are also required either to work or to spend time looking for work with the help of the center's employment counselor, to perform community service, and to participate in counseling groups meeting at the old jailhouse. When not pursuing these activities, they are permitted a level of freedom, subject to electronic monitoring, that increases with their successful adaptation to the program.

"I did it all—I robbed. I stole. I stuck up people," says Stan, a thirty-eight-year-old who had been a drug dealer and user for twenty-three years before his recent arrests. He credits the day reporting program for helping him stay drug- and crime-free after coming out of jail. "I do positive things and I stay away from the negative individuals. [Without] this program, I'd have been dirty when I got out. I'd have gone right back to using."

Day reporting in the United States began ninety miles due east of Springfield, in the Boston office of a nonprofit community corrections agency called the Crime and Justice Foundation. Looking for ways to help the state ease prison and jail crowding in the early 1980s, the foundation's program planners grew interested in day treatment centers developed in Great Britain. For the past decade programs in England and Wales had enrolled chronic offenders whose low-level criminality arose from substance abuse and a lack of basic life skills.

The centers were born of English and Welsh courts' frustration with the failures of both individual casework and incarceration in dealing with such people. As day treatment clients, they were required to appear daily at a single location for structured activities—social services, education, and recreation. In some respects the programs resembled those well established in the United States for juvenile offenders and the de-institutionalized mentally ill.

The Crime and Justice Foundation organized a steering committee of foundation and criminal justice officials that decided to open the first Massachusetts program at the Hampden County Correctional Center, which served the working-class cities of Springfield, Holyoke, and Chicopee in the western part of the state. Meanwhile Connecticut corrections officials had become interested in the British centers and approached the Connecticut Prison Association, a private penal reform group, to develop a pilot program.

As centers in Connecticut and Massachusetts developed and began to flourish, the idea spread. Hampden County regularly hosted visitors from jurisdictions all over the country seeking to set up day reporting centers of their own. A 1989 survey identified 13 day programs in the United States and another in Canada; a subsequent study completed in 1994 found 114 centers spread across twenty-two states. The growth reflected continuing concern over prison and jail crowding as legislatures mandated more incarceration, particularly for high-volume drug offenses. As they combined elements of accountability with treatment, the centers could serve as a practical middle ground between opposing views of law enforcement.

Corrections managers realized that day reporting centers could be opened relatively cheaply in storefronts or agency office buildings, with no need to go through zoning reviews and neighborhood confrontations. The concept also permitted agencies to design programs for special groups of offenders: the mentally ill, tuberculosis patients, stalkers, sex offenders, and recent graduates of correcitonal boot camps.

Day reporting sprang up in different forms, creating a definition problem. ABT Associates, the Cambridge, Massachusetts, research group that conducted the 1989 and 1994 surveys, found a number of elements common to the centers. They make a point of offering offenders enhanced access to social services. They manage supervision with frequent on-site contacts, off-site surveillance, and other measures such as drug treatment. And they typically move clients through "phases" as success in social service programs earns relaxed levels of control.

Otherwise programs that call themselves "day reporting" vary widely. Some are run by out-of-state corrections departments or parole agencies, others by county sheriffs, probation departments, and city jails. In some cases, the public agencies open and run the center themselves; in others, nonprofit groups develop the program and provide it under contract to the correctional agency.

The centers may serve as alternatives to prison when judges make them a condition of probation for offenders they would order locked up if the centers were not available; state corrections managers also use them as part of prerelease programming for convicts whose parole release dates are near. They serve as an alternative to incarceration for probation and parole violators; county jails may also seek to reduce crowding and promote rehabilitation by releasing inmates early to day reporting center programs. The 1994 ABT study of 114 centers found that 87 percent enrolled probationers; 73 percent took probation or parole violators, and 42 percent took parolees from prison. Thirty-seven percent enrolled pretrial detainees from county jails, and 25 percent accepted people released early from jail sentences. Twenty percent enrolled state prisoners on furlough or administrative release.

Jack McDevitt, head of the Center for Applied Social Research at Northeastern University, finds that programs fall along a continuum between supervision and services. Those that emphasize supervision, he says, may actually be no more than "a place to check in with your probation officer," whatever else they claim to offer, and such programs do little in the way of classification or screening.

The service-oriented programs at the other end of the spectrum set strict eligibility requirements and invest heavily in screening and classification; some then see their role mainly as placing offenders they have accepted in other programs in the community; some develop their own capacity for substance abuse treatment, employment counseling, and preparation for the GED exam.

The most recent ABT study is the only research to date that attempts to describe day treatment as it is practiced nationwide. The research, based on fifty-four responses to a survey questionnaire mailed to 114 day reporting programs, found them open five days per week or more, with average enrollments of eighty-five. One program had only fourteen clients, while at the huge Harris County, Texas, program—the nation's largest—more than 2,000 offenders per day participate at two locations. Established programs averaged 255 admissions per year.

The programs averaged one staff person for every seven clients, and costs averaged $35.04 per offender per day. In general, the survey found, day reporting centers cost more than regular or intensive probation supervision but less than incarceration or residential treatment.

The researchers found that offenders enrolled in day reporting programs fail to complete them at a high rate; many are then returned to jail or prison. On average, 50 percent of offenders are terminated from day reporting programs for negative reasons, though the figures varied widely by program—from 14 percent to 86 percent. The researchers found termination rates higher for programs offering more social services, apparently because such programs subject offenders to more rules and responsibilities, creating more ways for them to fail.

The ABT report concluded that day reporting programs "continue to be in a state of transition." More and more are being operated by public agencies, emphasizing surveillance over services, and being used as an enhancement to probation rather than as a way to remove inmates from jails or prisons. Even so, the study acknowledged the considerable potential demonstrated so far: "At this point, DRCs still occupy a unique position in the continuum of intermediate sanctions through their provision of both rigorous supervision and diverse services."

The Springfield, Massachusetts, program, which began by taking inmates from the Hampden County jail, makes clear that the centers remain a viable alternative to incarceration, however other jurisdictions may decide to use them. The 150 offenders enrolled for day reporting in Hampden County divide about equally between pretrial detainees and sentenced convicts (none is placed on the program as a condition of probation). The 75 sentenced inmates add up to the population of a "pod," or housing unit, of the county jail. In the program, they cost the county only $16.50 per client per day compared with $65.75 for a jailed inmate.

The fact that the Hampden County program's success is expressed in terms of jail, rather than prison, savings reflects the configuration of the correctional system in Massachusetts, where county jails hold inmates for up to two and a half years. Elsewhere, inmates convicted of similar crimes might be diverted to day reporting from state prisons.

The acceptance of day reporting in Massachusetts also reflects careful planning. Well persuaded that the English idea might work in the United States, the Crime and Justice Foundation and its steering committee produced a concept paper and circulated it to criminal justice leaders in order to build support. Legislators and judges appreciated the emphasis on a balance of supervision and service. "Members of the Massachusetts criminal justice community were receptive [to the day reporting idea] because it seemed to address overcrowding in a way that was politically acceptable to a variety of interests," reported a paper authored by McDevitt, Glenn Pierce, and Robyn Miliano. "The day center would be a community corrections alternative with a strong public safety element."

In the end, however, the program's successful launch depended most heavily on the selection of Hampden County as the place to begin. The sheriff, Michael Ashe, had been in office for 11 years and enjoyed wide popular support. On taking office he hired his brother, Jay, as superintendent of the Hampden County jail. The nepotism raised eyebrows at first, but any aroma of scandal faded as the criminal justice community and the public realized that the two brothers brought valuable experience to the job. Both hold masters degrees in social work from Boston College and had worked with juvenile offenders; their backgrounds had taught them how to combine tough pragmatism with a progressive willingness to innovate. Ethical inquiries didn't get very far, explains Elizabeth Curtin of the Crime and Justice Foundation, "because Jay is just so absurdly qualified."

Michael Ashe had run for sheriff in 1975 and won with a campaign in which he declared that his experiences with juvenile offenders had awakened him to the need for overall reform of criminal justice and corrections. He and his brother shared a belief in the importance of "sentencing people locally rather than down the road to the big house," Jay Ashe says. "You have an opportunity to impact them and recycle them back to the community as responsible citizens."

He adds that the opportunity to have such impact has increased with rising sentence lengths. Twenty years ago, jail sentences averaged six to eight months; today the figure is up to eighteen months. As that increases crowding, it also brings greater opportunities for rehabilitation and "recycling."

The Ashe brothers' reputation as reformers grew, and when the Crime and Justice Foundation went about setting up its steering committee to develop day reporting, Jay was an obvious candidate. That put him in a position to volunteer Hampden County for the pilot program when no probation department seemed eager for it. "We were managing scarce resources," Michael Ashe says of their decision. "I looked at [day reporting] as a positive thing."

The move caused some skeptical shaking of heads. "The rest of the sheriffs look at Mike Ashe," his brother observes, "and say, 'Hey, I don't get elected by having 150 guys out on day reporting and waiting for the phone to ring when one of those guys commits that heinous crime.'" A similar anxiety eventually tempered the brothers' enthusiasm. As opening day neared, Sheriff Ashe decided that the program should include a feature that is anathema to Curtin and her colleagues: electronic monitoring. She believed that probation departments reached too easily for ankle bracelets as a dubious technological substitute for supervision based on sound administration and human relationships.

"At the last minute, the sheriff got nervous about community reaction," Curtin says. "So he went out and announced [electronic monitoring] to a community group without telling anyone else. . . . The sheriff felt that people were not going to support it unless he had a real hot zinger to give them, and it worked."

Sheriff Ashe denies any last minute decision, however. Electronic monitoring, he says now, "was something we felt strongly about from the beginning . . . . We wanted the public to feel safe and assured." At the same time, he is the first to agree that the program does more to insure public safety with careful screening and solid management. "The real strength of the program is the selection process, the orientation, the ongoing supervision with the staff."

The episode reflects the sheriff's apparently well-tuned sense of the need for political shielding if programs like day reporting are to survive. "The sheriff has navigated that to the point where he is respected in the community," Jay Ashe says. "He goes out and sells it politically. He talks a lot out in the community, and the people trust and believe him."

That has helped the Hampden County day reporting program to survive and flourish for a decade. Since it opened in October 1986, more than 2,600 offenders and pretrial detainees have gone through the program; more than 80 percent of the sentenced cases and half the detainees have completed it successfully. The sheriff's phone has never rung with a call about "that heinous crime" committed by a convict out on day reporting. No longer an experiment, the program is well accepted as a constructive way to ease pressure on a crowded county jail.

For sentenced inmates of the Hampden County jail, day reporting begins as their release date comes into view. Those with six months left to serve may qualify if they survive screening interviews. For those with sentences of less than a year, consideration is automatic. Those with longer terms need a jail counselor's recommendation. Pretrial detainees are referred by judges with the help of a day reporting evaluator stationed in the courtroom.

A number lose out based on their record alone: no sex offenders, no violent offenses, no pending felonies, no active restraining orders (for spouse abusers), no drunk drivers who caused a serious injury or death. Interviewers then approach eligible inmates with 12 pages of questions. They go over issues of education, employability, family, housing opportunities while on day reporting. Previous failure in the program doesn't necessarily prevent another chance, or even several chances to see if the day reporting combination of supervision and services might finally have some effect. "We ask them what they think *they* need to make it on our program—not what we think they need," says Kathy Cumming, the day reporting intake coordinator.

The interviewers also try to assess the extent of an inmate's substance abuse problems and willingness to participate in therapy groups. Some are deemed good candidates for long-term treatment and transferred directly from jail to a residential drug program.

Before release to day reporting, an inmate must arrange for housing, usually with a sponsor (relative or reliable friend) approved by the program. A community corrections officer attached to the day reporting center makes a home visit to sign off on the residence itself and the sponsor's willingness to help with the client's supervision and support.

About 80 percent of those interviewed wind up enrolling. About 10 percent decline because they prefer jail to the demands of the program—which generally lasts about as long as the balance of a jail term. Others are turned down for lack of suitable housing or a sponsor willing to take them in, and some don't make it because they can't afford the telephone to which the electronic monitoring device must be wired.

The program's managers credit the heavy screening for much of its success—at the same time leaving themselves open to skeptics who say such "creaming" raises questions about its real effectiveness. Might not the carefully selected candidates who now make day reporting look good have done as well if simply released on parole? For now, the answer to this important question, while subjective, is usually "no." "It's my feeling that people would fail if they didn't have the support of the program," says McDevitt. That view is reinforced by clients like Stan, who readily expresses his gratitude for the fact that the program has kept him out of trouble.

For those enrolled, the program revolves around a simple idea: Structure and enforce a positive daily routine to supplant the aimless way of life that lets people run afoul of the law. The unemployed fill up their time with community service and treatment sessions. But the center invests heavily in putting clients to work in real jobs for real pay.

Richard Devine, the counselor who coordinates the employment effort, runs "job search" sessions with the unemployed two mornings per week. The clients comb the classifieds and go for job interviews. Devine also cultivates local firms willing to provide jobs. Some participate out of civic spirit, but many also find real advantages to hiring through the center.

"We're saying [to clients] you need to follow your itineraries, you need to be on time," Devine explains. "That's part of the same thing that the employer is looking for, . . . that you're going to work your scheduled hours and you're going to be drug and alcohol free. We do the Breathalyzer and urinalysis testing. So all those things are in place for the employer. . . . Instead of training somebody and a couple weeks later that person's gone, at least they know that they have the person for awhile."

Jim Galaska, owner of a stainless steel foundry called Trident Alloys, is one who read about Sheriff Ashe's project and offered to help. He has hired more than 20 center clients in the past seven years.

"We'll take a person and put him in the lowest wage job we have, sandblasting," Galaska says. "It's a dirty, filthy job, but it's a start. If they're willing to work, we'll promote them out of there."

Trident, he says, has not had a single bad experience with Devine's referrals. "Anything that's happened that causes them to go back in jail, it's something that's happened on the outside. The last time it was a guy who was driving without a license." To date, he says, more than 50 percent of the day reporting clients he has hired continue to work for the firm; one has earned promotion to foreman.

During their first two weeks in the program, clients and their counselors work out individualized "contracts" that detail their work, job search, community service, and treatment obligations. The treatment sessions run by the counseling staff focus on subjects like "anger management," "values clarification," "life skills," and "employment skills." The center also offers preparation for the GED exam and counseling for parents, couples, and family groups.

At the same time, clients are introduced to security routines. They are fitted for electronic ankle bracelets and told to expect visits from community corrections officers to install the monitoring unit. They also must begin to submit the itineraries that form the backbone of day reporting supervision.

Twice a week the client fills out forms detailing his or her exact whereabouts for several days in advance. The itineraries state when clients are to leave home, their destinations, how they will travel (walk, drive, take the bus, or get a ride), when they are to arrive, and when they are to return home.

The itineraries, McDevitt declares, may be "the single most important factor in making a difference to these people," because "most of them have never had to think about tomorrow. When the counselor says, 'what are you going to do tomorrow,' he says, 'I guess I'll go hang with the guys.' And the counselor says, 'Don't you get in trouble when you hang with the guys? Why don't you think about what else you could do?'"

The itinerary data is fed to computers that control the "programmed contact" monitoring system. Its telephone robots make silent calls to the clients' home monitoring sets. When such a call reveals that the client isn't in range, the computer follows up with a call that rings the client's phone. If at home, the client can reassure the computer by inserting a section of the ankle bracelet into the monitoring set. If the client doesn't answer, the computer prints out a violation notice at day reporting headquarters and notifies a community corrections officer's beeper.

Clients must report to the day reporting center each day and may be required to give urine samples for testing. When offenders find jobs, counselors follow up with employers and require that clients present payment stubs to verify that they are going to work. Each counselor is paired with a community corrections officer who conducts random visits to make sure clients are where they should be according to their itineraries. On such visits they will typically ask questions that might reveal new problems, administer a quick Breathalyzer test, and make sure the electronic monitor is working properly.

The officers are also dispatched to bring in clients found to have failed a urinalysis, been out of place for more than three hours, or committed other serious infractions. The unarmed officers have to rely on persuasion rather than force to make such arrests, but most errant clients go quietly as officers make clear that if they resist or run, they could be charged with escape and have months or years added to their sentences. Officer Genaro Medina recalls the case of a drunk who finally submitted to arrest after much belligerent discussion. "We told him, if we leave, you're going to get charged with escape." After the client sobered up the next day, Medina recalls, "he thanked us for bringing him back, because he knew that if we hadn't come back with him, he could have gotten another year and a half."

During the initial two-week period, clients are said to be in "phase one," the most restrictive. When they are not at work or participating in activities at the center, they are expected to remain at home, electronically leashed to the telephone, allowed out no more than one hour per week for church, and cannot be out of the house even for an approved activity after 8:00 P.M.

As they satisfy their counselors that they are following the rules and meeting obligations, they may advance through the next phases, each of which lasts at least four weeks. Higher phases grant later curfews and more time out of the house for shopping, going to restaurants, visiting friends, and a list of approved recreational activities. Much depends on availability of a phone to receive monitoring calls. At first, visits are allowed only with friends who have phones. Recreational activities must also accommodate community corrections officers who conduct surprise visits. Clients complain that they aren't allowed to play golf or go fishing, but the officers say they aren't about to spend hours searching a lake or golf course to complete a routine spot check.

Though 90 percent find jobs and more than 80 percent of sentenced offenders finish the program, not all find it easy. "A lot of them see this as being a whole lot harder than being in jail," says Mary Smith, a day reporting counselor. Day reporting requires that they participate in programs, while a jailed inmate who chooses to do so can just sit back and do time. Beyond that, the day reporting routine imposes unfamiliar demands. "You're leaving the house, you're coming down here for programs or going out doing community service, . . . you're responsible to report to someone."

McDevitt detects a clear pattern: "If they resist the temptations of freedom and don't fail within the first 48 hours, then there is a period where they do pretty well. Then after three or four weeks, they start to run into difficulty. The novelty has worn off; they still have to go to work every day, or if they're not working, the wife or girlfriend says, `Why are you hanging around the house?'" As the program is structured, however, counselors can use regular meetings to spot the early signs of such trouble and head it off.

For an offender like Jose, a fifty-four-year-old convicted of selling pirated videos, the program means two days of looking for a job and three days of community service that translates into janitorial work around the old jailhouse. He also has completed the anger management and family counseling programs. He complains that time for the job search program is too limited: "[B]y the time you get out there [for job interviews] it's almost time to come back." As for community service, he says, it's "the one thing nobody likes—no pay."

He found more to appreciate in the treatment programs. "I learned a lot. In anger management, I got to say things that I wanted to say." In the family program, he "learned about why some people act the way they act, coming from certain family backgrounds. It's good."

For Stan, the thirty-eight-year-old drug offender, day reporting takes a somewhat different shape, since he was employed as a dishwasher at the time of his arrest and his boss agreed to rehire him after his release to day reporting. "I go home, come check in, go back home, come check in, go to work. That's it." In addition to the support he gets in his effort to stay away from drugs, he appreciates the chance to keep his family together. "I've got a little newborn baby," he says. "By being in the DRC program with the bracelet, it gives you a chance to be home. You maintain the program and you can make it."

Frank, a twenty-nine-year-old with a history of alcohol trouble and a conviction on an explosives charge, expresses the most unalloyed enthusiasm. Before the program, he says, he was in "a really messed up cycle," where he would make money buying and reselling cars on his own, then "blow all the money" partying and "start all over again." After his release to day reporting, he persuaded a friend who owned a home security business to give him a job. Supervised by the program, he developed a taste for sobriety and steady employment.

"I've been working every day. I love it," he says. He recommends the program for "every person that comes out of jail. . . because the first thing you want to do when you get out is party. That would have been my first thing. I don't even feel like partying now."

Surprisingly, perhaps, the clients offer few complaints about the bulky ankle bracelet they must wear around the clock. "I forgot this thing the second day I had it on," Jose says. "To tell you the truth, I could live my entire life with that there. . . . Physically it doesn't bother me." Beyond that, clients are inclined to grant the system a fair measure of respect. "It works," says Stan. "You can step out of range and the machine will call you, and they'll know that you're out of range."

Tom Ashe, an electronic monitoring specialist for the program (and no relation to the sheriff), believes that few slip through the electronic net. Clients who flunk drug tests are likely to inform on others, he notes. "They'll say, 'I got positive for drugs, but Bob was smoking it too.' But I've never heard anybody say, 'Hey, everybody's messing around with their machines.'" Though more rigorous research could raise new doubt, the day reporting center in the old jailhouse now appears to succeed on the level of broader policy as well as operational detail.

"It's clearly a cost-effective program," Sheriff Ashe declares. Without it, he says, "the system would be backed up and I would be in a more severe overcrowding situation." He's hoping for even more relief as the county moves to use the program as a front-end option; judges would put offenders on day reporting as a condition of probation rather than sending them to jail.

"Absolutely it works," McDevitt says. "There's an expectation of a degree of service among the staff, a belief that this is what you do to do a good program."

Richard Devine and Yvette Cruz speak from the perspective of two who had worked in the main institution before taking their counseling jobs at the day reporting center. In the county jail, Cruz says, "We can give them counseling, we can give them programs and education, but while they are incarcerated, they don't have the opportunity to practice what they've learned."

In the institution, Devine says, "It was reactive. You waited for something to happen and reacted to it. Here, we're out there in the community, and we get to see people make it." He recalls the story of a client who returned to the center eight times before he finally straightened out. "He said, 'I'm getting old now. I'm 28.' It's been three years, and he's still clean; he's doing community service. . . . You don't give up on somebody. Who knows which time it's going to click?"

Drug Treatment
The Logic Is Overwhelming

FOR THE years of his late adolescence on the streets of New York City, the drug life agreed with Antonio. He easily managed his addiction to heroin and cocaine by selling enough of the drugs to support his habit and more. "When I was in the streets, I had it going for myself," the twenty-one-year-old recalls. The idea of entering drug treatment never crossed his mind. "I had the drugs, I had the money. I got what I wanted when I wanted it."

Then the law began to catch up. New York police mounted "buy and bust" sweeps, and Antonio got swept. The arrests and doses of jail time shook him up.

"Every time I got arrested, I thought about stopping—why am I in this game, you know? . . . But when I'd go back out, I'd go out and do the same thing again."

After his sixth arrest, Antonio met a man named Gilbert Acevedo, who spoke with unusual authority to young Hispanic addicts. As a police officer, he had become addicted to the same cocaine he bought and busted dealers for, got kicked off the force and gone through treatment. Now in recovery, he makes a career of counseling young addicts who wind up in court and in city jails. "He told me that I really do need help because I'd been to jail so many times," Antonio recalls.

Because his repeated arrests for drug selling put him in line for a stiff prison term, prosecutors found Antonio eligible for Drug Treatment Alternative to Prison (DTAP), a program that focuses on drug offenders headed for state penitentiaries. Now Antonio is drug free, completing school, and living in a therapeutic community run by Phoenix House, the operator of drug programs in New York and California.

That's good for Antonio; it also looks good for New York and all the other states struggling with prison populations swollen by crackdowns on drug-related crime. DTAP demonstrates the feasibility of serious drug diversion that remains credible with the courts and poses no threat to public safety.

The malignant relationship between drugs and crime by now seems beyond dispute:

- More than 50 percent of people arrested in American cities test positively for illegal drugs at the time of the arrest; in some cities the figure approaches 80 percent.

- More than 75 percent of jail inmates report using drugs at some point in their lives; 27 percent say they were under the influence of drugs at the time of their offense.

- Two thirds of state prison inmates say they have used drugs as regularly as once a week or more at

some time; more than a third say they were using
illegal drugs at the time of their offense.

• Two thirds of people entering residential drug
treatment and one third of those entering outpatient programs say they committed crimes for
economic gain in the year before they began
treatment.

Legislators' punitive responses to drug abuse, furthermore,
created new issues for courts and prison systems during the
1980s. At the beginning of the decade, violent crime accounted
for 48.2 percent of new commitments to state prisons, compared
with only 6.8 percent for drug crime. But by 1992 the figure for
drug offenders had more than quadrupled to 30.5 percent,
exceeding the 28.5 percent figure for prisoners convicted of violent crimes.

Depressing as it is, the continuing evidence that drug abuse
and crime are intimately linked also implies a reason for hope.
If addiction feeds crime, after all, then won't reducing addiction also reduce crime? And when it comes to treating addiction,
America's health care system is far from empty handed. Over
the years, it has developed numerous ways to treat addiction: short-term "detox" in a hospital followed by outpatient
therapy; methadone maintenance; drug-free counseling groups;
Narcotics Anonymous support sessions; intensive residential therapeutic communities where addicts live together and
address their drug problems in tough confrontational sessions.
Why not integrate these resources more fully into the criminal
justice process?

The obvious need has prompted varying levels of response
depending on jurisdiction. Some states make drug therapy available to offenders in prison, sometimes setting aside whole units
or prison complexes for treatment programs. Judges often make

participation in treatment—residential or outpatient—a condition of probation either for those convicted of drug offenses or for others who fail periodic drug tests while under supervision. Alternative sanction programs like boot camps, restitution centers, and day treatment centers include drug counseling of some sort as a part of the required routine. Residential programs run by nonprofit groups may accept referrals from the courts.

While there are powerful ethical arguments for helping destructively addicted people regain control over their lives, the most popular case for doing so depends more on common-sense economics. In some states, a year of residential treatment—the most expensive—still may cost only half what it costs to keep a person in a penitentiary for a year. On release, the penitentiary inmate is likely to go right back to a life of drug addiction and crime, imposing yet more costs on society, while the successful graduate of treatment may remain drug- and crime-free for years. The potential payoff far exceeds the incapacitation value even of several years in prison.

An eighteen-month study of addicts who had gone through California drug treatment programs found a 43.3 percent decline in illegal activity after participants had completed treatment. Researchers calculated a return of $7 for every $1 invested in treatment; the savings resulted from reduced crime and hospitalizations of the drug users.

Official attempts to take advantage of such economics stretch back at least as far as 1972, when the federal government funded a Treatment Alternatives to Street Crime (TASC) program through the Law Enforcement Assistance Administration (LEAA). The idea was to establish formal links between courts and drug treatment programs. The typical TASC agency helps courts identify offenders who could benefit from substance abuse treatment, diagnose their specific needs, and place them in the most appropriate programs. Then the TASC staff members monitor the offenders' progress, conducting regular drug tests, and report regularly back to the courts.

State and local criminal justice officials claimed big reductions in recidivism for TASC clients, and in 1976 Washington funded a rapid expansion of the concept through the LEAA. By 1978 the agency had spent $35 million to set up 73 TASC programs nationwide. When that money ran out in 1982, there were 130 programs in thirty-nine states. The programs have continued since then, supported by state and local funding, foundation grants, and client fees. Though their number had expanded to about 320 by 1996, the number of states in which they operated had declined to 30.

The programs vary from place to place. Some are free standing, while others operate as units of probation departments or public health agencies. Some run their own treatment while others contract it out to community-based providers; some take only lightweight first offenders while others enroll addicts with serious crimes or long records.

In 1996 a team led by M. Douglas Anglin of the U.C.L.A. Drug Abuse Research Center (the others were Douglas Longshore, Susan Turner, Duane McBride, James Inciardi, and Michael Prendergast), published a massive study of TASC funded by the National Institute on Drug Abuse. The findings were generally positive. The researchers interviewed 2,014 offenders in TASC programs and comparison groups in five cities (Birmingham, Alabama; Canton, Ohio; Chicago, Illinois; Orlando, Florida; and Portland, Oregon). They were able to locate more than 80 percent of the sample for follow-up interviews six months later.

They found that TASC participants benefited from more services than those in the comparison groups, who were either on standard probation or in other treatment programs. The TASC clients also tended to abuse fewer drugs less often, and they engaged less frequently in sexual behavior that exposed them to AIDS. TASC offenders in Birmingham and Chicago admitted to fewer drug-related crimes during the six month period. In Birmingham and Portland, however, the researchers found that TASC offenders were more likely to be arrested or to commit technical violations of probation than those in comparison groups. The researchers attributed this to the fact that the TASC programs subject clients to closer scrutiny. "From the standpoint of community safety," they write, "the greater likelihood of arrests and technical violations among TASC offenders might actually be considered a sign of success, not failure."

The researchers were impressed with the overall results. They had subjected the program to a rigorous research process, using conservative standards of comparison, and they noted that as a program often based on referrals, TASC would always be hostage to the availability and quality of programs where it operated. They emphasized TASC's continuing ability to make a positive difference despite huge changes during the 1980s and 1990s: the withdrawal of government funding for social service programs, the shift in drug abuse from heroin to crack cocaine, the increasing focus on punishment rather than treatment, the stresses of AIDS on medical and social service systems, and the disappearance of many blue-collar jobs.

Despite these adverse developments, TASC programs not only showed positive results but appeared to provide the greatest help to the most troubled offenders. "We believe the consistency of findings represents a strong signal of the effectiveness of the TASC model in different environments, with different client populations, and when tested in a highly rigorous research design," the researchers write. "The pattern of findings in this study suggests that the TASC model had favorable effects among offenders whose behavior was more problematic. . . . This is precisely the type of offender who is most in need of intervention and who represents the greatest recurring cost to the public."

The 1980s and early 1990s also saw an expansion of drug courts. The segregation of drug cases for special treatment developed as drug arrests, rising as police mounted crackdowns in response to public pressure, threatened to overwhelm court systems. Nationally, drug arrests rose by 134 percent between 1980 and 1989, though total arrests increased by only 37 percent.

The goal of the early drug courts was purely administrative—to speed the processing of drug defendants so that backed up cases would not clog calendars or crowd jails. Thus New York City established special courtrooms to negotiate quick pleas with drug offenders. Evaluations found that the new court sections succeeded in drastically reducing disposition time with only a slight decline in sentence severity.

Then in 1989 Miami opened a drug court with an expanded mission: To dispose of cases by moving offenders into drug treatment. The court accomplished this by deferring prosecution of drug addicts pending treatment and by dismissing charges of those who succeeded.

The program targeted relatively lightweight offenders and enrolled them in a course consisting of three treatment "phases." In the first, offenders report daily for drug testing at a county clinic until they achieve seven consecutive days of clean urine tests; in the second, they attend drug counseling sessions and fellowship meetings to maintain abstinence; and in the third they move to the campus of Miami-Dade Community College for GED classes and vocational training. The whole process takes a year or more, during which the judge keeps track of offenders' progress and may order backsliders to court for prosecution of the original charges.

The Miami court's effectiveness remains unclear. An American Bar Association group that studied it found that while the recidivism rate for offenders who successfully completed the drug-court program plunged from 60 percent to 7 percent, the court had little effect on recidivism rates of all offenders assigned to it, since many failed to complete treatment. But a subsequent study for the National Institute of Justice by John Goldkamp and Doris Weiland yielded more positive results. It found a rearrest rate of 33 percent for drug-court defendants compared with 53 percent for similar offenders before the court was established. It also found that for those drug-court offenders who were rearrested, an average of 235 days elapsed before the first rearrest, more than twice the length of time for other offenders.

The Miami drug court attracted much media attention during the early 1990s and won the endorsement of Janet Reno, who was serving as state attorney for Dade County before her appointment as attorney general of the United States. The concept caught on in dozens of jurisdictions around the country and gained a substantive boost with the 1994 crime bill, which authorized $1 billion for drug courts through the year 2000, with $29 million available in 1995.

By 1997, 151 drug-courts were operating nationwide and another 140 were being planned. They formed a new organization, the National Association of Drug Court Professionals.

While it is still too early to draw conclusions about the courts' actual usefulness, they surely afford some savings of jail bed/days, as they make a point of moving offenders into treatment quickly. An evaluation of the Oakland drug court after its third year found that its clients had 44 percent fewer felony arrests than those handled in the traditional ways.

Jeffrey Tauber, the judge who started the Oakland court, calculates that clients enrolled in 1991, the year it began, spent 33,869 fewer days in custody in the three years following their arraignments than the clients diverted under more traditional procedures the year before. The savings to the county on jail space and other law enforcement resources during the three-year period totaled $3 million.

Tauber emphasizes that "this stuff is not easy." A successful drug court, he says, "requires a different view of the system, a different view of the offender, and a different view of how to deal with the various participants in the system. . . . It's hard to get people working together when they're most interested in protecting their turf and their resources. . . ." Someone has to exert leadership, he says, "to break down the obstacles to cooperation and start building linkages."

TASC and drug court administrators invest a heavy measure of faith in the idea that offenders ordered into drug treatment by a court will do as well as those who enroll voluntarily. Daily experience of treatment providers appears to confirm that they will, though the research community has yet to buttress the impressionistic evidence with more than suggestive findings.

The two most respected studies were published in the late 1980s. One examined a group of drug users ordered onto methadone maintenance under California's Civil Addict Program. These addicts were compared with a group also committed to the program but then discharged because of legal problems with their commitment. The legal errors made possible a validly controlled study. The addicts who remained in treatment showed reduced levels of drug use and criminal activity over a follow-up period of eleven to thirteen years.

The second survey, known as the Treatment Outcome Prospective Study, or TOPS, followed 11,000 people enrolled in various types of drug treatment. The study found that addicts referred to treatment from the courts stayed in treatment longer than those enrolling for other reasons, and more of them stayed drug free for longer periods after release. The study also found that the positive results were the same for those ordered to treatment by the courts and those who responded voluntarily to a court referral.

While these are impressive findings, they are based on addicts who mostly were using heroin in the 1970s—a more benign time than the crack-cocaine plagued 1980s and 1990s. Newer studies cast doubt on the effectiveness of legal coercion for modern addicts. Though none is considered definitive, some have found that factors other than the reason for entering treatment have more effect on the treatment outcome; others show that legal coercion is simply not a factor in retention or other favorable outcomes.

In the meantime, promoters of drug diversion argue that ordering offenders into treatment remains worth doing so long as they do no worse than if they were incarcerated for a similar period. Treatment providers point out that it may often take several attempts before an addict succeeds with a treatment program. The idea that even those who fail retain some benefit from the treatment experience lends weight to the argument for integrating it as a regular element of criminal justice even in the absence of statistics documenting dramatic success rates.

Charles Hynes, the Brooklyn District Attorney, started DTAP shortly after his election to succeed Elizabeth Holtzman in 1989. A durable fixture of New York's political and legal communities, Hynes continued to reside in the Flatbush section of Brooklyn, as he had all his life. "The reason I ran in 1989 had very much to do with the fact that I had become a crime victim," Hynes explains. "My house had been burglarized four times in five years. Two of my cars were broken into more times than I cared to report. Three of my five children had been assaulted."

On taking office, Hynes quickly grasped the link between crime and drugs. In the years between 1975 and 1989, the percentage of drug-related crime in the city soared from 15 percent to an appalling 75 percent and continued to climb. Hynes also knew something of treatment, as he served on the board of Daytop Village, one of the city's leading independent nonprofit drug treatment providers. The logic seemed clear: Identify nonviolent drug-involved offenders and divert them into treatment programs.

Hynes recruited Susan Powers, an attorney who had dev-eloped pilot programs for the Vera Institute of Justice. About that time, she had been reading the Treatment Outcomes Prospective Study with its findings about the effectiveness of court-ordered treatment.

"The idea was to start slowly, achieve some measure of success, then convince government officials to expand it." Hynes says. Friends and colleagues were dubious. "People said, `What if somebody leaves the program and murders someone?. . . What are you getting yourself into? But I decided the thing was worth a try."

Other numbers, after all, were seductive. Residential treatment, the most expensive mode, still cost only $18,000 per client per year, while each drug offender sent to prison might cost the taxpayers $44,000 annually—$29,000 for six months in a city jail followed by $15,000 for the rest of the year in state prison. Beyond that, Hynes found research showing that each nonviolent drug addict might commit 10 crimes a week to support a habit. Taking 100 addicts out of crime and putting them into treatment could prevent 50,000 crimes a year. "It could be a real reduction in crime," he says. "It could have an impact on the quality of life—on the people who were breaking into my car."

Powers convened meetings of all the players—judges from the city's drug courts, prosecutors and defense attorneys, drug treatment providers, probation and corrections officials—to explain the program and gain support. The idea met with suspicion.

Defense attorneys, for example, found it hard to believe that a program originating in a prosecutor's office would actually try to keep defendants out of prison. They worried that DTAP would become just another form of "net widening," a dumping ground for weak cases. But Powers explained that this time prosecutors were genuinely worried about that, too. They wanted diversion that produced real savings on jail and prison costs. They decided to focus the program on offenders who have a prior felony conviction as well as a real drug habit. New York law mandates prison time for the second felony; there was no question that diversion of two-time felons would create a true alternative to incarceration.

Rather than ask the legislature for an exemption to the law, Hynes and Powers used their discretion to defer prosecution and drop charges for addicts who successfully completed treatment in a nonprofit-run residential drug treatment center. Those who failed faced aggressive prosecution—with no deduction of the time spent in treatment from an eventual prison term. This too reinforced the alternative-to-prison idea, since prosecutors, knowing they could be back in court with a defendant who failed at treatment, insisted that only those facing the strongest, most winnable cases be allowed into DTAP.

Treatment providers also hesitated. They weren't prepared to make any special allowances for court-referred clients, nor were they willing to impose any special rules the prosecutors might require. Treatment, they felt, depended on the integrity of the communities they had in place, and why should they do the DA's any favors? Their waiting lists for clients from the community were already yards long.

With the help of a group called Legal Action Center, the two sides negotiated a deal. For the most part, the agencies would treat a DTAP client the same as any other. They retained the power to reject a client at the beginning and to expel any who broke the rules. While prosecutors could pursue clients who were expelled or left treatment on their own, they had no power to interfere beforehand. An enrolled offender's status in the program remained the sole business of client and provider. The programs agreed, however, to notify prosecutors immediately once a client had left.

The drug-court judges brought up their concern: that the screening and other paperwork necessary to enroll a defendant in DTAP would gum up the works of a court designed for the speedy processing of drug cases. DTAP promised to complete all the preliminaries within five days. Finally, DTAP negotiated agreements with probation and parole officials to defer revocation hearings for the many clients who qualified for DTAP but were already on probation or parole when arrested.

Though lengthy and often frustrating, these initial "open planning" meetings turned out to be a crucial factor in the program's eventual successful launch. They created, Powers writes, "a reservoir of good will and mutual trust . . . all the participants felt that they, too, 'owned' the program."

The DTAP process begins with the prosecutors' identifying eligible cases: people truly addicted to drugs, charged with a second felony, but with no violent offenses on their records. As a practical matter, most turn out to be the hapless harvest of police undercover operations, people who were observed selling drugs or are charged with selling them to officers.

The prosecutors disqualify addicts who won't provide information making them easy to track down—a verifiable home address, names and addresses of relatives and friends. Those who survive that screening face a second one with the drug treatment providers. Of all those the prosecutors first identify as eligible, one third rejects a chance at the program themselves (most decliners insist they are innocent or that they don't have a drug problem); a second third doesn't meet providers' requirements for admission (usually because of severe psychiatric or medical problems); and the final third enroll for DTAP. As they do, they are required to waive their rights to prompt indictment, speedy trial, and confidentiality.

To reassure judges and the public, DTAP offers another unusual feature: its own dedicated enforcement team. Defendants might easily walk away from the nonsecure treatment programs, and inevitably some did. When a program reported such a disappearance, prosecutors immediately went to court for an arrest warrant. But everyone, including defendants, knew that the police department's warrant squad was so overworked that capture remained a remote possibility. Powers therefore hired some retired police and corrections officers to find errant DTAP clients and bring them back to court. Diversion to treatment would not become a first step to escape.

The program finally opened for business in October 1990. By 1995 with the active support of state substance-abuse treatment and criminal justice agencies, it had been replicated by prosecutors in other boroughs of New York City, and its capacity citywide had grown to more than 300 clients.

All the offenders are sent to cooperating residential treatment programs that follow the therapeutic community model. Living together, members of the group pursue courses of study or job training in addition to cleaning and maintaining the house. They also enforce rules and participate in individual, family, and group therapy meetings. The process emphasizes total honesty to the point of tough confrontation in group sessions and generally seeks to mobilize the power of the community to heal the individual.

Successful clients eventually advance to a "re-entry" phase where they spend more time away from the house and work on finding employment or schooling and a support network for life back in the real world. Well persuaded that employment is crucial to holding down recidivism, Hynes set up a Business Advisory Council to help graduates of the program find jobs. DTAP also plans to send clients in re-entry to work as trainees for a company that provides food service for government-funded agencies.

The process can last two years or more, another convenient fact for DTAP managers wary of a skeptical public. Felons convicted of similar drug selling are likely to serve about the same amount of time in prison.

So far, DTAP has earned solid praise in the criminal justice community, commendations from politicians, a favorable press, and only a few complaints. There haven't been any real disasters—no clients escaping to rape, maim, or murder. ("It hasn't happened, but I'm not going to discount the possibility," Hynes says, fingers crossed). Anecdotally, at least, the program demonstrates daily the importance of legal coercion to the treatment process.

The best witnesses to that are the clients themselves. "Being arrested was what got me here," a thirty-five-year-old addict named Jake responds directly when asked what brought him into

treatment at Phoenix House. "I wouldn't in my wildest imagina-
tion have believed that I would ever be in a place like this." Though
drugs and alcohol had been a factor in his life since childhood—he
smoked his first marijuana at the age of nine—he had also managed to function well from time to time, graduating from high
school, completing two years of college, holding straight jobs. But
the choice of state prison or DTAP was no choice at all, and he
never found any reason to regret his decision. "Phoenix House is a
very beautiful place," he says. "Either you grow, or you go."

Others come with the idea of "jailing time"—faking their way
through the program in order to avoid the discomforts of incarceration. Therapeutic communities are hard to fool, however,
and those who try to skin by wind up in harsh confrontations
with their peers. "I came to the program to get out faster,"
admits Henry, a forty-seven-year-old who traces his drug habit
back to Vietnam. "But I've learned to deal with myself."

Chris, age thirty, agrees that he didn't know what he was getting into when he accepted treatment as an alternative to prison.
He credits the threat of jail for keeping him on a successful track.
"If I wasn't mandated here, I would have left a lot of times," he
says. "I had my bags packed on the third day, because this was
hard." Treatment, he asserts, "is harder than jail, but it's worth
it. The longer you're here, the better it is."

Both clients and managers of therapeutic communities suggest that critics exaggerate the idea that addicts ordered into
treatment by the courts may be less motivated than those who
come on their own. "Very few come here because of a big real-
ization that they are dysfunctional and need help," says John
Blette, a regional director of adult programs for Phoenix House.
While "some come because otherwise they would be in jail, others come because their families have pressured them into it."

Defense attorneys share the basic positive view of DTAP. The
deferred prosecution, they say, offers a major advantage over
TASC programs that enroll clients after conviction. DTAP "does

help people turn their lives around," says Carolyn Wilson, an attorney with the city's Legal Aid Society. "For people who get accepted into it and complete it, it's wonderful. They get their case dismissed, and as predicate felons they would be prison-bound if they had any kind of conviction or plea."

But Legal Aid has also had some complaints about eligibility. At first, says Russell Neufeld, a Legal Aid supervising attorney, DTAP went along when providers refused to take clients who were pregnant, did not speak much English, or had AIDS. Now all are accepted, but only after the defense lawyers pressed the constitutional issue. "Once treatment became a DA's program, a state action, you had an equal protection situation," Neufeld explains. "It's all changed now, but these were fights."

The lawyers still object to DTAP's policy of requiring offenders to make quick decisions about whether to take the treatment option, often in the attorney's first meeting with a strange client. "The guy is still either high or in withdrawal when you are trying to talk to them about it," Neufeld explains. The offender may have little understanding of what treatment entails and be leery of the two-year commitment. Powers insists that clients have a second chance to sign up a few days later, but Legal Aid attorneys claim that many assistant district attorneys haven't gotten that message. In any case, permitting defendants too much time would violate DTAP's pledge to judges that it will process diversions quickly.

The lawyers also fault DTAP for its unwillingness to place a defendant in a second program should he or she be expelled from the first. TASC has no such rule and routinely makes second placements when circumstances warrant. Neufeld points out that therapeutic communities operate according to strict rules and will expel clients for fights over trivial matters or for violating a ban on romantic relationships. "We've had clients thrown out because they fell in love," Neufeld says.

"The point of this is legal coercion," Powers responds. Success depends on clients remaining in treatment even when it becomes uncomfortable. Too much generosity with second chances sends the wrong message. To that extent, she admits, there certainly is a conflict between coercion and treatment, especially when providers and researchers confirm that it may take a few attempts at treatment before a person really can be helped.

DTAP's enforcement team underscores the intended message on a daily basis. Led by a former state parole officer and a former assistant deputy warden in the city jail system, the team verifies the offenders' home addresses and other contacts as a condition of acceptance, then pursues those who abscond.

"We don't discriminate against a person because he doesn't have a home," explains Fred Weinberg, the former parole officer. "Individuals are creatures of habit. If they say they are homeless, we ask, `Where are you homeless?'" In one case, they verified that a client lived in a car on Pitkin Avenue in the Bronx. When he left treatment without permission, the team found him soon enough, back in his car.

For clients who don't make their lives so easy, the team relies on standard detective work, persistently questioning relatives and friends, and developing informants in the neighborhood. While some leave because they weren't serious about the program, many simply miss their families, especially mothers separated from their kids. "They forget sometimes that they still are defendants," Weinberg observes.

By April 1997, DTAP had found 2,652 defendants eligible, and 1,758 of them had opted to participate. The screening process eliminated 966, leaving 792 to enter treatment programs. Of these, 276 completed treatment and another 151 remained in the programs. Of the remaining 365 who either dropped out or were expelled, 95 percent were either apprehended by the teams or returned to court by other means. Those figures are good enough to make a statement in a city where the police department's general warrant squad is hopelessly overworked. "The word is out that there is a special warrant team," Weinberg declares.

DTAP managers claim a one-year retention rate of 64 percent, much higher than drug treatment programs in general. The recidivism (post-treatment arrest through July 1995) rate was 19 percent for DTAP graduates, compared with 46 percent for a group found eligible but that elected not to participate. (By April 1997, the DTAP recidivism rate had declined to 11 percent.) Those figures compare with a recidivism rate of 40 percent for New York City felony drug offenders who go to prison.

Only 24 percent of those opting for the program wound up graduating or currently participating in it, a factor that in one sense dilutes the claim of successful treatment. But unlike other programs, DTAP isn't vulnerable to charges of "creaming." Figures for October 1995 confirm that DTAP provides real diversion of serious offenders: Of the defendants who refused to participate or were screened out, 78 percent were either convicted of a felony and sent to prison, entered felony pleas, or had been indicted for a felony. Of those who left the program, 82 percent were convicted of felonies and sentenced to prison.

Whatever their promise, the numbers remain too small to effect any real savings on jail and prison space. Hynes talks of a major push in the state legislature for an expansion of DTAP to 5,000 clients or more, a scale that eventually might begin to reduce prison costs. The problems of creating space and developing staff, not to mention general uncertainties about state and federal funding, remain significant. But the payoff could also go well beyond the state budget.

"There is nothing better than to talk to a client who succeeds with the program," says defense attorney Alan Abrahamson. "Before, he's like a deer caught in the headlights; he can't engage in a conversation. Afterwards, he can engage you in a conversation about his life. Nobody has ever benefitted from doing prison time for selling crack on the street."

Sex Offender Treatment
When Prison Provides No Answers

TENSION FILLS the air in the small room, and discomfort clouds the faces of the eight men seated about on sofas and chairs. Even so, all insist that they are glad to be here, and they mean it—even Sam, who has begun a long confession.

His life is in tenuous shape right now. He's on parole after serving several years in prison for raping a woman, and he's been granted home visits with his wife and kids. But an angry outburst on a recent visit escalated to the point that his wife's landlady notified his parole officer, who suspended his visiting privilege. Now he's filled with remorse.

Along with the other men in the room, he's come to understand a few things about himself—in his case, how deeply his problems are anchored in old pain, the years of being teased and bullied as a kid, the humiliations and rejections by women as an adult. He continues to struggle with a deep-seated diffidence that in middle age seems reinforced even by his physical appearance: slight build, buck teeth, and not much chin. Instead of fighting back, his habit is to push the anger down inside until one day it all comes out at once. That's how he gets in trouble.

He realizes what he did wrong. He'd felt the outburst coming on. But instead of talking about it with someone, he tried to hide from it once more, keep his secret, isolate himself, afraid to confide in anyone.

Now, finally, he's talking. "I'm afraid to be alone. I'm afraid if I say something wrong to my wife she's going to take off. So I don't say what's really bothering me. I stuff it."

"You're still the person that raped that woman," the therapist, Gary Allen, comments. "You're still being secretive . . . . You're not dealing with your emotions up front. . . . What will it lead to this time?"

Then it's the others' turn to weigh in.

"Great hindsight, Sam," says Bud, who comes to the group after serving time for molesting his teenage daughter. "But we've been down this road with you a couple of times. You admit to it after it's happened, but you don't believe it. . . I know how that works. That's me. . . Has it sunk in, that you can talk to people, you can trust people?"

"Yes," Sam says, nodding and closing his eyes. "Yes it has."

Sam, Bud, and the six other men show up weekly at Allen's office in Burlington, Vermont, as participants in a statewide program that provides treatment for sex offenders. The program, a unit of the state corrections department known as the Vermont Center for Prevention and Treatment of Sexual Abuse, demonstrates the usefulness of such therapy for much more than its clients. It offers some hope that offenders once considered beyond help no longer need to generate frustration for criminal justice or pose continuing danger to their communities.

To the general public, to the news media, and quite often to themselves as well, sex offenders are the worst people in the world.

Their crimes range from vicious sexual assaults, compulsive pedophilia and incest that require incarceration for the sake of public safety, to conduct that seems more offensive than physically dangerous—drunken groping and exposure. Whether violent or only distasteful, such behavior requires a mental-health response that isn't always available or accessible. And since it usually violates the law, the nation's courts and correctional systems wind up having to deal with sex offenders for better and worse.

During the 1980s the task increased. Arrests for sexual offenses (other than prostitution) totaled 44.6 per 100,000 in 1980; by 1991, with victims more willing to report sex crimes, the number had risen to 59.3. In 1979 the number of sex offenders in state prisons was estimated at 17,053, or 6.2 percent of the total state inmate population. By 1992 the number had swelled to more than 76,000, or 9.8 percent of the total, and appeared to be still climbing. In individual states today, the numbers are even higher. In Washington, for example, the figure is 25 percent of an inmate population totaling 10,830. In Vermont, sex offenders account for 22 percent of 1,350 prisoners. In Pennsylvania, the figure is 14 percent of 28,000 inmates.

Even so, there appears to be no national consensus on how to respond. Some states continue with therapy programs, but a number of others, facing tight budgets, have recently scaled back programming or abandoned it altogether.

The troubled history of efforts to treat sex offenders dates back to the 1930s, when psychiatrists began recognizing "paraphilias"—the catch-all term for urges that underlie pedophilia, sadomasochism, exhibitionism, and other sexual misconduct—as symptoms of mental disease that might be cured. States began passing "sexual psychopath" statutes permitting diversion of offenders to the mental health system. Thirty-one legislatures approved such laws from 1938 to 1966.

By the 1970s, however, researchers had begun to puncture the confidence that underlay the psychopath laws. Some studies found that most sex offenders were not suffering from serious mental illness. Others found that treatment had no apparent effect on recidivism. All the while, the public continued to crave real punishment for sex crimes; treatment sounded too soft.

As a result, state after state gave up on diversion to the mental health system and resumed sending sex offenders to prison. By 1990 only five states continued to operate under the old sexual psychopath laws.

At the same time, however, mental health and corrections officials, well aware that incarceration hardly reduced recidivism either, continued to explore new modes of treatment. These efforts drew support from research confirming widespread sexual victimizations. A national study found that 27 percent of women and 16 percent of men had been sexually abused as children. A Los Angeles study found that 13.5 percent of women could expect to be raped at some point in their lives.

Treatment of sex offenders therefore continues: For offenders deemed dangerous and sent to prison, it may begin while they are still behind bars and continue after parole release in community outpatient programs; others are sentenced directly to community-based treatment programs run by private providers and public mental health agencies. A national survey conducted by the Vermont-based Safer Society Program, which promotes treatment for sex offenders, counted 1,784 programs for adult and juvenile offenders and for child victims of sexual abuse.

The number of programs for offenders had more than doubled between 1986 and 1994. The society found 123 residential programs operating under the auspices of courts or prisons and another 54 court- or prison-related community outpatient programs. They ranged in scale from Pennsylvania's, which enrolled about 1,000 inmates in twenty-two institutions, to New York's, which provided treatment for 52 in a program at one prison and for another 150 or so in groups scattered around other institutions.

In the state of Washington, a program for 400 offenders grew
out of the legislature's enactment of a determinate sentencing law
that took effect in 1984. State officials realized that the end of
parole under the determinate sentencing plan would mean the end
of discretion to release sex offenders doing well in treatment while
keeping those most likely to reoffend locked up for as long as possible. As a result, the legislature created the Special Sex Offender
Sentencing Alternative, or SSOSA, to incorporate treatment into
the new sentencing process. First offenders found to be amenable
to treatment have their felony sentences suspended in favor of a
short dose of jail followed by up to three years of treatment with a
private therapist under corrections department supervision.

In nearly every state, the available programs appear to fall far
short of the need. According to one national count, only 11,200
of 85,000 prisoners classified as sex offenders in 1993 were getting any treatment. Thus even Pennsylvania's large effort serves
only about a quarter of the state prison inmates convicted of sex
offenses. In Washington, the SSOSA program can deal with 400
offenders, and an in-prison program treats 200 more. But those
numbers account for less than half the total number of convicted
sex offenders in custody or under supervision.

Ongoing research and clinical practice offer dozens of ways to
deal with paraphilias. They fall into three broad categories:

- Group therapies designed to effect "cognitive
  restructuring," or changes in offenders' patterns
  of thinking and feeling.

- Use of drugs to reduce testosterone levels or
  relieve obsessive compulsive disorders.

- Aversive conditioning, or behavior modification that subjects offenders to mental or physi-

cal discomfort as they become aroused by visual
or auditory depictions of deviant sex.

Clinicians may combine some or all of the therapies in programs they design for individual clients. Many currently favor a
concept known as relapse prevention, based on the belief that
total cure of deviant urges deeply embedded in the psyche may
be impossible. Offenders, the theory goes, still can learn to render their feelings harmless by managing them as they would a
chronic condition, such as asthma or diabetes.

Powerful conflicts emerge when sex offender treatment gets
integrated into the criminal justice system. In order to succeed,
therapists need the freedom to invade the most intimate areas of
a man's inner life (virtually all of those arrested for sex offenses
are men), sometimes in ways that seem offensive or bizarre.
Criminal justice agencies, meanwhile, remain bound both by
their obligations to observe offenders' constitutional rights and
to protect the public.

Civil liberties questions arise when behavior modification
therapies become a de facto condition for a favorable parole recommendation. Do procedures that appear to use a new form of
abuse to quench old abusive feelings violate basic human rights?
Does making parole dependent on them coerce the offender?

Tales of excess haunt the field: inmates given emetics so that
they vomit while viewing pictures of deviant sex, or hooked up
to the penile plethysmograph (a device attached to the penis to
measure sexual excitement), then subjected to mental or physical torture as they are inappropriately aroused. "Homework
assignments" requiring offenders to masturbate while taping
their fantasies raise issues of privacy.

Jerome Miller, a psychiatric social worker who treats sex
offenders in the Washington, D.C., area, warns that behavior
modification in the hands of therapists working for criminal justice agencies can easily turn abusive. "The pioneers of psychi-

atric social work didn't feel it should get associated with the criminal justice system," he points out. "And there's a lot of truth to that." But other practitioners insist that punitive and extreme procedures are rare.

A second area of conflict concerns the confidentiality of a client's statements during therapy. Offenders, especially some pedophiles, may have committed many more sex crimes than those that resulted in their conviction. Owning up to them, coming to terms with the past, becomes an essential part of the therapeutic process. But what should therapists do with such information?

For years the therapists could assume communications with clients were privileged, not to be disclosed without the client's permission. But as concern grew about child abuse, states began passing laws mandating the reporting of sex offenses against children. These laws took precedence over the therapist-client privilege. While intended to expose more cases, stop the abuse, and get help for the victims, the laws often had the opposite effect, as offenders aware of the trouble that might ensue stopped talking so freely in therapy.

Dr. Fred Berlin, Martin Malin, and Sharon Dean studied the rates at which patients at the Johns Hopkins Sexual Disorders Clinic disclosed cases of abuse after Maryland's legislature tightened its law in 1989 to require reporting of child abusers' confessions in therapy. Between 1979 and 1989, 73 patients had entered therapy to talk about their abuse of children. With no disclosure law in effect, none was prosecuted for the abuse they revealed. But in many cases, the abuse ended, the patients left jobs that put them in contact with children, moved out of homes where they had been abusing children, and started taking drugs to reduce their sex drives and help control their behavior.

After 1989 not a single new adult not facing criminal charges referred himself for treatment because he had sexually abused children. No children at risk were identified as a result of the law.

Instead, the researchers write, the law "appears to have deterred honest disclosure by patients in treatment and to have deterred unidentified potential patients from entering treatment."

Even so, such laws remain a fact of life for most therapists working with sex offenders today, and that sometimes leads to tormenting frustration. Miller tells of a call from a man who said that he had raped his daughter and that now they were having sex regularly. "He realized that they both needed help, but I said, 'If you come in, I'll have to report you.' He never came in."

The third big area of conflict concerns the relationship of the recovering offender with the rest of the world. During the 1980s parole officials began running into difficulty with communities that objected when released offenders who had committed gruesome violent crimes tried to move in. News of sensational crimes committed by paroled sex offenders put the focus on them.

In 1990 Washington became the first state to pass a law that ordered released offenders to register with their county sheriffs and gave the sheriffs authority to notify the public about offenders they found to be dangerous according to a set of guidelines. A New Jersey law enacted in 1994 *requires* notification of the public about released offenders local prosecutors find to be "high risk." The federal crime law enacted in 1994 authorized mandatory registration of offenders with police, who may notify communities about dangerous cases. In 1996 President Clinton signed a federal law making community notification mandatory as well.

The effects of such laws remain to be seen. In New Jersey, officials found themselves coping with misdirected anger and confusion when addresses offenders had listed turned out to be wrong. Administering the law properly, they found, would take more resources than they had imagined, in order to keep track of all the released offenders and verify information to be made public. In Washington, sheriffs did not complain about administering the law, but a 1993 survey found that neighbors harassed 14 of

176 offenders who became the subjects of notification. Offenders were threatened and assaulted; in the worst case, an arsonist set fire to an offender's house. In New Jersey, notification apparently prompted two neighbors to burst into a house looking for a released child molester and to assault another man by mistake.

Concerns about notification are perhaps deepest among therapists trying to help sex offenders continue with their treatment after release. Sex offenders, they say, are most likely to reoffend when they come under the kind of stress notification seems designed to impose. Berlin points out that it is helpful for offenders in treatment "to reintegrate into the community, to have jobs, have friends. If we are going to publicly brand people, ostracize them, then the laws intended to be helpful may actually turn out to be harmful."

Despite these difficult issues, the need for some sort of sex offender treatment as a part of criminal justice remains a source of continuing concern. Beyond the ethical case for helping offenders deal with deviant sexual obsessions, treatment appears to be the most sensible approach to protecting the public, in terms of economy as well as safety. The public costs of a reoffense may easily exceed $100,000 for prosecution, years of incarceration followed by parole supervision, and services to the victim. Sex offender treatment, meanwhile, may be the least costly to taxpayers of all the alternative programs. Sex offenders are likely to be much more affluent than, say, drug addicts, and may plausibly be required to pay for much of their own treatment themselves.

The total (rather than annual) cost of treatment for an offender in Washington's SSOSA program, for example, is $19,642, of which offenders pay 60 percent, or $11,785, leaving a public cost of $7,857. That compares favorably indeed with $45,717 for the average twenty-seven month prison term without treatment and $55,923 for prison with treatment, for which the state

picks up virtually the entire cost. (The savings are offset somewhat when offenders flunk out of treatment, have sentences
revoked, and return to prison to serve their full term, as happens
in 17 percent of cases.)

The arguments for treatment, of course, only hold up to the
extent it succeeds. Recent studies provide a basis for optimism
despite the negative conventional wisdom.

The prevailing skepticism stems from a landmark review of
research published in 1989 by Lita Furby, Mark R. Weinrot, and
Lyn Blackshaw. They examined recidivism studies in North
America and Europe dating back as far as the 1950s and concluded "that there is no evidence that treatment effectively
reduces sex offense recidivism." While critics of therapy programs seized on the study to attack them, many failed to read it
carefully. For the authors made clear their belief that the review
did not confirm ineffectiveness of treatment so much as the failures of research.

Sex offenders are more resistant to accurate recidivism study
than other kinds of criminals. Nearly all experts believe that the
vast majority of sex offenses go unreported; studies that count
only rearrests or reconvictions are a poor gauge of reoffending.
Yet inducing offenders to self-report actual rates of reoffending
engages big issues of ethics and law, not to mention credibility.

Researchers also face special problems when putting together
groups of sex offenders for comparative studies that would yield
meaningful results. The ideal study would match offenders in
treatment with those who seek help but are denied it. But is it
ethical to reject those who want treatment? What liability would
that create in the event of new offenses by those rejected? As a
result, many studies depend on questionable pairings of offenders given treatment with less comparable groups.

Finally, Furby and her colleagues acknowledge that many of
the studies they reviewed were of treatment modalities long considered obsolete or irrelevant. They also note that some of the

studies date from a time when people were regularly arrested and prosecuted for consensual adult homosexuality, conduct now legal or decriminalized nearly everywhere in America. Their study concludes not with a discrediting of treatment but a call for better research: "Progress in our knowledge about sex offender recidivism will continually elude us until adequate resources of time, money and research expertise are devoted to this issue."

In the years since the Furby article appeared, other studies have confirmed the effectiveness of newer approaches to treatment, especially those based on relapse prevention. One conducted by the Solicitor General's office of Canada reviewed recent research and found a number of reports that plausibly documented reduced recidivism. For example, it found three "cognitive-behavioral" programs whose graduates had a sexual recidivism rate of 10.2 percent, compared with 25 percent for comparison groups. A study of violent sexual offenders who underwent treatment showed a reconviction rate for any offense (including nonsexual and nonviolent crimes) of 22 percent, compared with 54.5 percent for a comparison group.

"A reasonable conclusion from the available literature," the Canadians concluded, "is that treatment can be effective in reducing sexual recidivism from about 25% to 10–15%."

Another study was conducted by Margaret A. Alexander, director of sex offender treatment for the Wisconsin corrections department, as a direct response to the Furby group's paper. Alexander reviewed 74 research reports and found an 18.5 percent recidivism rate for untreated offenders, compared with 10.9 percent for those who got treatment. Her paper documented improved effectiveness in recent years: Offenders involved in studies conducted before 1980 recidivated at a rate of 11.9 percent, compared with 8.4 percent for those in treatment studies conducted after that year. And those who underwent newer programs based on the relapse prevention model had a lower recidivism rate

(10.7 percent), when compared with those whose treatment involved only behavioral and group therapies (15.4 percent).

The Vermont Center for Prevention and Treatment of Sexual Abuse (VCPTSA) enrolls 48 sex offenders in prison and another 325 on prison furlough, probation, or parole. That's a substantial contribution in a small state: Men convicted of sex offenses account for 300, or 22 percent of the 1,350 sentenced to Vermont's crowded prisons.

The program provides a valuable alternative. Before it began in 1982, recalls Judge Paul S. Hudson, who sits on the state district court in Windham County, "prison would have been the automatic response," even for the less serious sex offenders. "All you could do was incapacitate them for a few years, then let them out, older and meaner."

As it diverts men from prison or gets them paroled early, VCPTSA saves the state a substantial amount of money. It costs Vermont more than $20,000 per year for an offender in state prison (in-prison treatment for sex offenders adds about $5,500). But a year of outpatient treatment, for which offenders pay on a sliding scale based on income and insurance, costs the state only $346.

The program might not exist at all were it not for a tragic coincidence. In 1979 Vermont used money from the federal Law Enforcement Assistance Administration for a task force to study what to do about sex offenders. As the group was issuing its report in 1981, a sensational rape-murder case put the whole issue on the front page. Two twelve-year old girls were abducted while walking home from school. Both were raped and beaten; one died, but the other survived to identify the assailants. "It put Vermont into a tailspin," recalls Georgia Cumming, a member of the task force who now serves as the program's coordinator of offender services, "because it was such a brutal offense, and then when they apprehended the two assaulters they ended up being fifteen- and sixteen-year-old boys."

Had the murderers been adults, the result might have been harsher punishments for sex offenders, but the soul-searching over fifteen-year-olds raping and murdering twelve-year-olds helped prod the legislature to approve a residential unit for 16 prisoners that began as the Vermont Treatment Program for Sexual Aggressors. The corrections department recruited William Pithers, a psychologist from the University of Rochester, to run the unit.

Before long, the need for an outpatient program became obvious—"It occurred to us that these guys were going to be getting out," Pithers says. So he recruited therapists to run the follow-up groups, arranging for guaranteed payment of $3,000 per group per year. He also set up joint meetings with probation and parole officers responsible for offenders to reassure the therapists about supervision. Judges soon began sentencing some offenders directly to outpatient treatment as a condition of probation, and the Treatment Program for Sexual Aggressors became the Center for the Prevention and Treatment of Sexual Abuse.

Today, Pithers directs nine in-prison therapists and administrators plus a network of 24 therapists running 40 outpatient groups. To be accepted for treatment, an offender first must survive an initial assessment. The program won't take murderers, career criminals, or offenders who mutilated their victims. It also rejects those suffering from a major psychiatric disorder. Offenders have to admit to their sex crimes and persuade the staff that they are genuinely motivated for treatment.

Once accepted, they are introduced to the principles of relapse prevention. Pithers claims to be the first to use that model, familiar in the treatment of substance abuse, for sex offenders. In an article describing their work, Pithers, Cumming, and three colleagues (Linda Beal, William Young, and Richard Turner) explain the treatment process. The therapist begins by emphasizing to the offender that he may never be rid of his urges for deviant sex; his goal instead is to learn to control them. To do that, he first needs to identify "precursors" to offending. A list of the most common such preoffense emotional states includes feelings of generalized anger, anger toward women (for rapists), depression, boredom, workaholism, and low self-esteem.

In the next stages leading up to an offense, the offender may fantasize about abusive sex, then turn the fantasies into "cognitive distortions"—rationalizations that make deviance seem acceptable. The rapist believes that all women crave violent sex; the father who abuses his daughter thinks he is giving her appropriate sex education; the pedophile tells himself young boys desire sex with him and are skilled at the arts of flirtation and seduction.

In such a state of mind, the offender makes "apparently irrelevant decisions" designed to make it possible. A rapist fights with his wife or girlfriend, then goes for a drive and picks up a female hitchhiker. A pedophile gets bored and depressed, goes for a walk, and winds up on a park bench near a schoolyard. The task of therapy is to help the offender understand the distortions of his thinking, confront the deep feelings that get him going in the wrong direction, and increase his awareness of the seemingly unconnected decisions leading to trouble.

Through this cognitive-behavioral therapeutic approach, the angry man learns to express anger appropriately rather than holding it in until it erupts; the depressed man probes the sources of his depression. Both learn to watch their behavior carefully when they feel angry or depressed. And should their "lapses" progress to the point of getting in a car or going for a walk in a dangerous emotional state, they are supposed to recognize the peril they are in, step back from it, and seek support from others.

Offenders work on these issues in therapy groups, and also with "homework assignments" between sessions. Some of these are based on workbooks published by the Safer Society Press that lead the offender through an extended process of mental and emotional self-examination. Other assignments require that offenders masturbate while tape recording vocal fantasies about healthy and deviant sex. The idea seems grotesque, but Pithers emphasizes that the tapes produced by such activity become a powerful tool in subsequent group therapy sessions.

Most offenders in prison and some of those working with therapists on the outside also submit to a tougher form of behavior modification. These "olfactory aversion" treatments require offenders to listen to audio tapes describing sexual activity and receive whiffs of ammonia when a penile plethysmograph registers excitement. (Originally the program used suggestive photographs, but that practice had to be abandoned when outsiders questioned the use of slides depicting children and Pithers found that not all were accompanied by valid releases.)

Though critics continue to question the use of phallometry, Pithers insists that it is benign. The procedure is done, he says, only with informed consent after extensive discussions with the offender to assess his problems and see if it might help. A monitor independent of the corrections department stands by to make sure the explanations of possible dangers are complete.

To protect the public from possible "relapses," the outpatient program devised an elaborate plan for an "external, supervisory dimension." The centerpiece is called the "network of collateral contacts"—selected family members, friends, employers, or others who can help keep an eye on the offender's behavior. He is required to explain the full circumstances of his offense and his particular precursors for reoffending to all members of the network. They are introduced to his probation or parole officer, who checks out what the man has told them. The offender is expected to report lapses to members of the network, but also to talk with them generally about how he's managing, all with the understanding that the network can and will pass along everything it hears.

The program keeps offenders who have succeeded with the in-prison program on a short leash. Granted furloughs 60 or 90 days before their parole hearings, they are permitted to live in the community and required to continue with outpatient therapy. Their daily schedules are planned to permit little free time, and they are supervised closely.

Should they continue to do well, the good conduct gives prison officials another reason to recommend their parole release. But since they are still on furlough, still legally in state custody, they can be yanked back to prison immediately, with no need to go before a judge or the parole board, should their network begin reporting lapses and their therapist give a negative assessment of progress in the group.

Two cases described by Pithers and Cumming suggest how the collateral networking and the furlough release procedures can work together to protect both the program and the public.

In one case, a rapist took a job at a corner store where he discussed his history of offending and his risk factors with his boss and his coworkers. One day, it fell to him to unload a new shipment of magazines and put them on a display rack, and some of the magazines turned out to be pornographic. A serious risk factor had dropped right into his hands. But because everyone in the store understood the problem, he was able to ask a female coworker to trade the task of unloading the magazines for work that she was doing, and she was glad to oblige. The man reported the incident to his therapy group, winning praise for good risk management.

Another case was more disturbing. A man convicted of sexual assault went to work in a restaurant. While stacking supplies in the basement, he noticed an open door to the room where waitresses changed into their uniforms; looking in, he saw a woman wearing only her underwear. He thought of approaching her, but then thought better of it because if she rejected him, he might begin fantasizing about rape. Though he did nothing more at the time, the peeping constituted a lapse, which he had to report to his therapist. When the therapist told him to come up with a strategy for avoiding another such lapse, he went out and bought a lock for the waitresses to put on their door.

The man's treatment team grew concerned: Instead of working on his own feelings and behavior, he had come up with a response that made it the waitresses' responsibility to protect themselves from him. A call to the man's employer with an innocent question about how he was doing set off another alarm: The man was the most diligent he had seen in years, the restaurant manager said. He was now even spending hours of his own time down in the basement rearranging supplies! The treatment team quickly pulled the man back to the in-prison program for another dose of training in relapse prevention.

How well does the program work? The most recent evaluation, conducted in 1991 by Vermont's Agency of Human Services, found that of the 473 offenders who had participated in outpatient treatment from 1982 through March 1991, only thirty were believed to have reoffended. The recidivism count included not only new arrests and convictions, but also therapists' and parole and probation officers' suspicions of new offenses never reported to police.

The overall recidivism rate of 6 percent compares favorably with other studies of sex offender recidivism, but the evaluators made no effort at a rigorous comparison with a matched control group. The evaluation also showed much lower recidivism for treated pedophiles (7 percent), incest offenders (3 percent), and men who committed "hands off" offenses like exposing themselves (1 percent) than for rapists (19 percent). But even the high rate for rapists looked good compared with the 38 percent rate of recidivism documented by an earlier study of untreated offenders.

While such figures suggest that the VCPTSA has developed a sound working model, they leave open a big question: to what extent do managers of the program predetermine a good outcome by selecting only those offenders likely to do well in treatment? Pithers acknowledges that the 38 percent figure comes from a group of men who got no treatment because they refused it themselves, were turned down, or flunked out of the program. "Clearly they're not a comparable sample," he agrees, since they obviously lacked the motivation of those who succeeded in therapy.

Even if the program does favor the easier cases, however, its positive effects on them, not to mention the potential victims of the reoffenses they won't commit, are impossible to dismiss.

The best witnesses to that are the offenders themselves. "All the different things I've learned since I've been in the program are what helps me day-to-day," says Jake, a child molester who comes to group with Sam and Bud. "If I start going in the wrong direction, if I get a whiff of danger, there are stop signs now, there's a thing that goes off in my head that says no. It never said no before."

Residential Restitution
"They Have Reason to Work"

THE LONG evening of drink and drugs put the boys in a wild mood, and sometime after midnight they saw their first chance to act on it: a hapless homeowner's late model pickup, standing in its carport, keys in the ignition. They pushed the truck quietly down the driveway, then drove it away, parked it, and smashed its windows with rocks. The taste of destruction tapped into a deep thirst for more. Before dawn broke, they had invaded a portable classroom unit of the local school and set it ablaze.

The judge gave two of the boys a dose of prison for the crime, but he couldn't see his way to it for a third, Michael, a troubled lad of nineteen who had mostly been along for the ride. The judge let the boy off with a sentence of probation, stiffened by a hefty restitution order: $7,500 to cover his share of the considerable damage.

Michael didn't appreciate the favor. Within a few months, he was in trouble with the law again, arrested on a marijuana charge. That sent the case to a probation department hearing officer. In another time and place, he might have shrugged off Michael's youth and problems and recommended that the judge send him to prison.

But South Carolina, like a few other states, provides another choice. That's how Michael wound up working every day for five dollars an hour in a plastics plant. Three quarters of every paycheck goes for court fees, fines, and the restitution payment. More gets taken out for room and board at a residence on prison grounds, where Michael and a few dozen other "restitutioners" occupy cement block cubicles.

The program "wants you to work," he says with a sigh. "They want their money, so you've got to work."

The idea of restitution as a sanction for criminal behavior goes back at least as far as the Old Testament. Scholars point out that while the biblical sentence guideline of "an eye for an eye, a tooth for a tooth," conjures barbaric images, its intent was to measure retribution: The victim deprived of an eye or a tooth should seek no more than an eye's or a tooth's worth of punishment in response.

In medieval Europe, a person convicted of a crime could "buy back peace" with a restitution payment to the victim along with a fine to the local lord. Anglo-Saxon kings put price tags on injuries—a man who cut off another's ear might settle the matter with a restitution payment of 30 shillings; for knocking out an eye, the amount was 66 shillings. In tenth-century France, a criminal could be sentenced to do a victim's work and pay him money.

As national governments began extending their influence over local justice, court-ordered payments more often went to the state than directly to victims. To recover precise amounts for losses and damages, the injured resorted to the civil law. Restitution no longer played a big role in the criminal courts.

In the 1970s, however, U.S. courts began to acknowledge the

needs and concerns of crime victims, and restitution experienced a renaissance. Where judges simply made it a condition of probation, leaving enforcement up to overworked probation officers, collections lagged. Officers resisted the extra work and offenders lacking job skills weren't able to produce that much income in any case.

But federal funding for local criminal justice encouraged formal restitution programs, especially for juveniles, set up to help offenders find jobs and ensure that some of their weekly pay would go to victims. Liberals and conservatives alike could support an "accountability" model of justice that imposed the discipline of work on wayward youth in lieu of harsher but less productive punishment. By the early 1980s, Federal officials could count 85 restitution programs for juveniles operating in 26 states. A 1978 survey, meanwhile, had found 87 restitution programs for adults nationwide.

Programs took different forms, in some cases aspiring to become real alternatives to incarceration rather than new wrinkles for probation. Some allowed offenders to live at home but helped them find work and established a routine for regular restitution payments. The Victim Offender Reconciliation Project, developed in the Midwest by Mennonites, arranged for meetings of offenders with their victims to ventilate feelings and negotiate a contract for the restitution amount.

Still other programs were residential; offenders could go out to work each day but had to live at a restitution center. Residents typically were required not only to work but to remain drug and alcohol free, get along with the rest of the group and participate in substance abuse treatment and other classes. Failure to meet these obligations constituted a probation violation that risked a short spell in jail or years in prison. The residential programs were especially interesting as they offered round-the-clock supervision of offenders that judges might otherwise not consider good probation risks. They held down staff costs as they took advantage of the employer's supervision, free of charge, during hours the offender spent at work.

Restitution continued to expand through the 1980s, mostly in the juvenile courts. A survey published in 1987 counted 221 programs set up to help offenders find work and confiscate a portion of their earnings for payments to victims. Some of these programs overlapped with community service efforts, as they required participants to contribute some labor to public agencies or nonprofit groups in addition to holding down a paying job. In a few cases, restitution programs put jobless clients to work for local government—cleaning parks, washing police cars—so that they could make payments to victims.

Research revealed problems. A German scholar, Elmar Weitekamp, reviewed North American restitution programs in the 1990s and cited haphazard planning, implementation, and evaluation; infrequent use of restitution as a genuine alternative to incarceration; restriction of the sanction to property and first-time offenders; and inconclusive evidence about the effects of restitution on recidivism.

Others pointed to incomplete payment. New York State's Division of Criminal Justice Services found that by the end of 1989, offenders had paid only 27 percent of the $92.3 million ordered in restitution since 1985. A 1994 survey of all offenders with restitution orders in North Carolina found that 46 percent paid no restitution at all, 41 percent paid in full, and 13 percent made partial payments.

Officials of seventy-five programs responding to a national survey in 1991 said that 67 percent of offenders paid their restitution amount in full, but when the researchers took a close look at four of the programs, they could confirm full payment for only 42 percent, and those, they noted, were programs chosen because they were well run. Not surprisingly, interviews with 198 crime victims found a low rate of satisfaction with restitution.

In some places, however, restitution still succeeded in establishing itself as a useful alternative sanction. A Pennsylvania

judge, Lois Forer, sitting in the Philadelphia Court of Common
Pleas, grew interested in the possibilities for restitution during
the 1970s and took it upon herself to impose the sentence
instead of jail or prison. Weitekamp reviewed 173 of her restitution cases between 1974 and 1984 and found that more than 60
percent successfully completed their sentences. These cases came
to the judge without the prior screening common in more formal
programs; many who wound up with restitution sentences had
committed serious offenses involving violence. "Weapon use,
whether an offense was a crime of violence or a property crime,
gang membership and victim injury, made no consistent difference in whether Judge Forer imposed prison or restitution,"
Weitekamp writes.

Many such offenders would clearly have gone to prison if not
put on probation with a restitution order. Yet their relatively
good performance on probation, especially in light of recidivism
statistics for people coming out of prison, meant that "the
increased use of restitution did not lead to heightened risks to
public safety." Weitekamp concludes that "the results support
wider use of restitution for more serious offenders than is now
the case."

Elsewhere, the mounting costs of incarceration stirred interest in
restitution as a cost-effective option that could be sold to the public. In 1983, for example, a Texas legislature feeling pressure from
the federal courts to reduce prison crowding authorized restitution
centers where convicts would reside while going out to work for
private employers or to perform unpaid community service.

During the 1980s, Texas opened 16 of the centers for an average daily restitution population that approached 500. Though
some of the centers offered substance abuse treatment and other
services, promoters of the program depicted it as inexpensive
punishment rather than community-based rehabilitation. The
law required that offenders be employable and that they be legitimate candidates for state prison.

Richard Lawrence, who examined records of 717 offenders admitted to seven of the Texas centers during fiscal 1987, confirmed that they were working as a genuine alternative to incarceration. Assessments of the 717 found 53 percent rated at the maximum risk level and another 37 percent at the medium risk level. During the year they earned a total of $1.14 million, of which they kept only $43,511 in savings accounts. The rest went for room and board, restitution, family support, debt payments, and court fees.

Even so, the Texas centers showed high failure rates. Of the 717 offenders studied, 453 were discharged from centers during fiscal 1987, but only 141 left because they had successfully completed the program. Nearly twice as many, 270, left because their parole was revoked for disciplinary violations. (An additional 41 transferred out for other reasons.) Figures for all sixteen centers for fiscal 1993 showed that of 1,872 discharged during that year, nearly half left either because they absconded or otherwise violated the rules.

On balance, however, Lawrence found that the centers met the goal of cost-effective diversion from prison. The daily cost of a bed in a restitution center was $27, compared with $33 for a prison bed, before the capital cost of constructing the cell. (The centers, operating in leased space, had no capital cost.) And the centers did not appear to pose any new threat to public safety. More restitutioners had their probation revoked than did a sample of offenders released on parole, but most of the parole violators committed new crimes, while the vast majority of restitution failures were for breaking center rules or other technical violations.

"Results show a significant number of offenders diverted from prison, a high rate of employment among the residents, and a considerable sum of money collected," Lawrence writes. "The study shows that a state with a high incarceration rate and a large, crowded prison population can successfully divert a significant number of offenders to restitution centers at no greater risk to the community."

The state of Georgia runs an older, even larger program consisting of eighteen centers with a total capacity of 1,029. In 1994
the probation department admitted 3,595 convicts to the centers, enough to have some impact on prison crowding and
costs—especially since a Georgia prison bed costs $48 per day to
operate, while one in a restitution center costs only $26.

The first centers opened in 1973 for restitutioners only, but as
diversion became a buzzword with the legislature, the probation
department rechristened the places "diversion centers" and gave
up the requirement that only those owing restitution could participate. Even so, Vince Fallin, who served as superintendent of
the first restitution center and today heads the state's probation
division, says that more than 90 percent of diversion center residents are working off fines or restitution orders.

He claims a better success rate than Texas; some 75 percent of
diversion clients, he says, complete the program in good standing. The centers are part of a long menu of escalating intermediate sanctions in Georgia; in terms of seriousness, they are a step
up from house arrest with an electronic monitor and a step
below the state's probation detention centers, where inmates are
subjected to higher security.

The diversion center, Fallin says, is "one of the most popular
alternatives available to the judiciary. The judges really, really like
it." A center "gives a person some structure, it focuses on work,
it's less costly than prison, and it gets them away from their home
environment for a while. It meets all the needs the judiciary has."

South Carolina's first restitution center opened in Columbia, the
state capital, in 1987; three years later, a second opened
in the industrial city of Spartanburg, in the northwest corner of
the state. Both are housed in nonsecure buildings on the grounds
of state prisons.

The centers were created by an Omnibus Criminal Justice
Improvements Act, which explicitly authorized the restitution

program as an alternative to incarceration in state penitentiaries. State criminal justice officials had long recognized the need for a structured restitution program with access to employment, since many offenders facing restitution orders could not pay because no jobs were available in their communities.

The law limited the program to nonviolent offenders, who would serve up to six months in the restitution centers for offenses carrying sentences of a year or more, up to ninety days for those with sentences of less than a year. Judges could send offenders to the centers as a condition of probation, on a suspended sentence, or after revoking probation. In 1988 the legislature also approved commitment to a restitution center as a condition of parole. The law said residents could be required to perform up to fifty hours of work per week; center managers insist that all residents perform the maximum amount. Those with paying jobs for fewer hours per week make up the difference with unpaid community service.

South Carolina probation officials modeled the daily routine on Georgia's. Sentenced offenders spend a week or so being evaluated by the social work staff and finding jobs. Full time job developers at the centers recruit employers and make placements. Offenders ride to work in vans provided by the center if no public transportation is available. Those who go to work, remain drug and alcohol free, and otherwise obey the rules may qualify for home furloughs of up to thirty-two hours. They can also earn shorter passes for shopping or going to the movies.

Each center has places for forty-eight men, plus twelve women at the Columbia center and fourteen at Spartanburg. They eat and attend classes together, but sex is strictly forbidden on site.

Employers send paychecks directly to the centers, where an accountant deducts 75 percent for payment of restitution to victims, court-ordered child support, fines and court fees, and room and board at the rate of $6.50 per day. The offender has access to the remaining 25 percent to cover carfare (the center charges $2 per round trip for rides in its vans) and a personal allowance of $15 per week. Any remaining funds go into savings accounts; offenders with clean records at the center may withdraw up to 50 percent of the balance for personal use, to pay family bills, and to cover medical expenses, for which they remain personally responsible.

As of September 30, 1995, 2,327 offenders had been admitted to the centers, which had collected a total of $3.8 million from their paychecks. A resident who works for six months at a minimum-wage job can expect to pay off between $3,000 and $4,000 in restitution and fines. When restitution orders exceed that amount—some residents have arrived with obligations of $10,000 or more—the offender goes home after six months but continues on probation and is responsible for finding work at home and continuing to pay. The impracticality of that leads some judges to say the legislature should extend the six-month limit.

When not at work or on an approved furlough, offenders are required to stay at the center, where they are supervised by correctional officers from the state prisons nearby. The centers offer long menus of social service programming: substance abuse treatment groups, money management classes, GED instruction, discussions of anger management, parenting and life skills. Offenders may be ordered to participate in one or more as conditions of probation, but work comes first. The need to work overtime or switch to a night shift takes precedence over class attendance.

Despite a rocky start, the program works well today. South Carolina's Department of Probation, Parole, and Pardon Services, having never managed a residential program, tried contracting out the task, first to Volunteers of America (VOA) and then to the state corrections department. Neither arrangement satisfied Michael Cavanaugh, who headed the Department of Probation, Parole, and Pardon Services until January 1995. The VOA, he says, didn't manage the program rigorously enough, and he found that the philosophy and working approach of corrections officers clashed with those he wanted for a probation-based program.

In 1993 Cavanaugh hired Thomas Scott, a county jail administrator, to take over management of the centers for the probation department—with good results. "When you have two big agencies trying to run the program with two different philosophies, you tend to have a lot of problems," says Joy Thompson, director of the Spartanburg center. "Now everyone's under the same umbrella."

From his little office in the old warden's residence that houses the Columbia Restitution Center, John Boron runs what amounts to a medium-sized employment agency. In the five years he's been in the job, he's cultivated enough fast-food outlets, upscale restaurants, auto repair shops, landscapers, and other labor-intensive enterprises to guarantee all his clients quick placement. "Our people . . . are working within ten calendar days," he says. "Generally, it's five days."

The great majority work at menial jobs for the minimum wage, but when clients arrive with valuable skills, Boron tries to place them to their advantage. He shows a visitor a daily roster that includes an iron worker and a concrete finisher working for $10 per hour along with the $5-per-hour placements at McDonald's. Higher earnings mean an earlier payout of restitution and release from custody.

The clients present special challenges. "I have a fantastic mechanic who can't read or write," Boron says. "Who is going to hire you if you can't read the spark plug gaps?" He placed the man with a Midas Muffler shop, where repetitive work could be performed without any need to read. Another client, asked about work experience, boasted of his success selling drugs. Boron found him a job selling cars.

Employers present certain problems as well. Boron had to give up on retail chains like Walmart and T.J. Maxx because they have inflexible policies of never hiring convicted felons. And he had to write off the hundreds of jobs for waiters and waitresses in the area because so much of their income gets paid off the books, in tips. That creates a temptation to cheat that can't be ignored. "I had two young ladies working for the same restaurant, the same shift," he laments. "One was turning in $5 a week in tips, and one was turning in $35 to $40 a night."

Employers who qualify, however, begin to depend on the restitution centers as a reliable source of labor and have been known to give restitutioners permanent employment once they complete the restitution payments. The manufacturing plants around Spartanburg are chronically troubled by high turnover or workers who show up only sporadically for low-wage, repetitive jobs that offer little chance for advancement. Managers are more than willing to take advantage of the extra motivation supplied by a judge.

"They have reason to work," says Ron Robinson of North American Film Company, a producer of plastic garment bags for dry cleaners. "We know they're going to be here, and the ones I've seen have been hard workers. . . . They have restitution they've got to pay."

In addition, the center makes sure the client has a way to get to work—Boron has three vans and ten drivers running workers to and from job sites around the clock—and tries to keep them sober and drug free. The center's staff also helps with discipline.

"I've developed a very good rapport with employers," says Linda Sinkfield, the Spartanburg job developer. "I try to talk with them at least once a week to see how our people are doing." Ruby Cromer, office manager for Personnel Solutions, Inc., a temporary help agency, recalls the case of a client from the center who rebelled against work and decided to call in sick. After Sinkfield took the man aside for a sharp "a word of prayer," he returned to work "transformed," Cromer recalls.

Her agency, which recruits workers for local businesses, credits the center with making it possible to stabilize the erratically staffed second and third shifts at a plastics plant. "What we had run into was a lot of turnover," she says. "It's hard to produce a quality product when nobody's ever seen one because it's their first day." When restitution center vans full of people ready to work began showing up regularly, the manufacturer was impressed. Restitutioners now account for half of the people on the evening and night shifts. When they pay off their restitution and leave, the plant managers ask for replacements from the center. "It's the first choice for openings that come up," Cromer says.

The centers' social service programs reinforce and facilitate the employment process. "Our motto is, we're here to help you get through this," says Betty Sheriff, the Spartanburg supervisor of social services. "We live with these people. We can see their patterns." She estimates that a quarter of the center's population has mental health problems, and nearly all the rest have problems with drugs or alcohol.

The gamut of programs covers substance abuse, domestic violence, GED preparation, victim awareness training, and "cognitive behavioral" skills. A visiting psychologist helps with assessments and referrals to the department of mental health for serious therapy. But Sheriff also finds herself handling a lot of individual issues with motherly heart-to-heart advice.

Problems include "anything you can think of," Sheriff says. Beyond the substance abuse, restitutioners typically have problems with managing anger and learning how to communicate with others. Commonly, she intervenes on the spot rather than conducting regular therapy sessions.

How well does she see the program working? "It's like a lot of other things," Sheriff says. "You take away what you're willing to take away." She estimates that "a third probably aren't going to do it; a third will talk you a good job, then go in the bathroom and smoke marijuana on the weekend; and the other third actually are trying and are going to make it."

The percentage of successful cases might be improved, she

and virtually everyone else involved with the centers agree, by a serious program of aftercare for clients who continue to need the kind of support and advice available at the center once they return home. As it is, those who can't earn enough to pay off their restitution amount in six months go back on regular probation, where opportunities for job placement, substance abuse treatment, and other social service help are far less certain.

"Some of them come here and they are the perfect resident for six months," Thompson says. "Then as soon as they leave the structured environment. . . they get in trouble and get arrested."

While some experienced convicts complain that steady work and the center's rules make for harder time than prison, others obviously appreciate the chance the program represents.

"It's not that bad," says Michael, paying for the night of destruction with his buddies. "You make a lot of friends. You learn how to get along with people, how to hold your aggression back." The disciplines of group living and regular employment "make you think about a lot of stuff you ain't ever thought about before."

James, a thirty-eight-year-old drug addict working to pay off $4,200 in bad checks and court fees, explains his willingness to follow the rules. "I know that if I mess this up, I'm looking at a lot of time. . . . It's a pretty good motivation to do the right thing."

"I kind of wanted to come here," says twenty-seven-year-old Jimmy, who led police on a drunken highway chase that ended when he tried to smash through a roadblock, totaling two police cars along with his own. The alternative was an eight-year prison sentence. "They told me, `You come out here and do six months, you stand a chance of getting off probation . . . getting your license back. All you've got to do is prove to us that you're sober, you're trying to straighten up. . . .' If it wasn't for this place, I don't know where I'd be."

Some also acknowledge the help they are getting. "A lot of the staff members took a great interest in me," says Veronica, a twenty-four-year-old crack addict whose troubled family relationships led her to steal $4,000 from her father's liquor store. "Ms. Sheriff, she's just the perfect mother." She adds that her minimum-wage job at the plastics plant has taught her something about the work ethic as well.

"I can work now," she says. "I'm all right with it. About two years ago, I wouldn't have worked in a pie factory. I just didn't want to work. Now they've taught me that you've got to work, that I can. That's a lot of good. That's going to carry me for the rest of my life."

Such responses have persuaded enough South Carolina judges and prosecutors to favor the centers as a sentencing option that the waiting list for places in them exceeds a month and can be as long as three months. Some judges consider them most useful as · an alternative to prison for technical violators of probation.

"If I have the restitution center available, then I don't revoke a guy's suspended sentence and put him in jail for six months," declares Judge Costa Pleicones.

Judge Thomas Hughston declares that "in many cases I use it as an alternative to incarceration," and he is glad to do so. He recalls sentencing in a case before the restitution centers opened.

Two men pled guilty to burglarizing the home of an old man who didn't trust banks; the burglars made off with a safe that contained the man's life savings, $50,000. The money was never recovered. "I gave them twenty-five years in the penitentiary," the judge recalls, "but it didn't do anything to get back this man's life savings. I'm sure he would have preferred a way to get his money back. He lost his life savings and all I could do was send them to prison for 25 years."

The only outside evaluation of South Carolina's restitution program so far came from a State Reorganization Commission whose findings remain problematic. In two reports, one issued in 1991 and the second in 1993, the commission insisted that "the Restitution Center Program is not being used to divert offenders from prison as the S.C. General Assembly intended, but is instead 'widening the net of social control' by placing additional constraints on offenders who would have received probation." However, in its second report, the commission found a "true diversion rate" of 35.5 percent plus another 10 percent whose diversion status "could not be determined"—figures that hardly support the idea of egregious net widening.

Furthermore, the commission based its negative view of diversion on figures for incarceration of those who failed for disciplinary reasons, arguing that anyone not sent to prison after ejection from the program probably would not have been sent to prison in any case.

The program's defenders challenge the basis for that assumption and dismiss the commission's evaluations as shallow and simplistic. In a response to the commission's first report, in 1991, the Department of Probation, Parole, and Pardon Services asserted that "no one can truly say, yet alone measure, what would have happened in the absence of program 'X.'" The probation agency "does not feel that it is valid to make a post hoc analysis of the state of mind of the sentencing authority, either at a first or subsequent hearing." In any case, the agency adds, the fact that not all who go to restitution centers would otherwise have gone to prison say more about how judges choose to use them than about their value as genuine alternatives.

There is no question that a restitutioner who goes to the center costs the state less than if he or she had gone to prison, but the amount is hard to determine with any precision. With their social service and job development staffs, in addition to administrators and guards, the centers are relatively expensive to run— the daily cost per restitutioner totals $27.78, only about $7.00 less than the cost of a day in prison after deducting the restitutioner's contribution to room and board. But restitutioners may spend many fewer days in the center than they would if they had gone to prison. As a worker, furthermore, the restitutioner pays taxes and generates money to compensate crime victims and to support his or her own family.

"No attempt can be made to assess the totality of benefits which accrue to the individual and the community," the Department of Probation, Parole, and Pardon Services writes, "when a 'prison-bound' offender succeeds at the Restitution Center, goes on to complete supervision, and re-enters society as a law-abiding citizen."

That sounds good enough to Cliff, sent to the Columbia restitution center after violating probation on a larceny charge. He's spent much of his thirty-nine years in state and federal penitentiaries for a number of property offenses, and he managed to put at least some of his time inside to constructive use by learning meat cutting. Boron found him a job cooking at an Appleby's restaurant, and he suddenly finds he loves to work for a living.

"I enjoy it," he says. "We broil-cook on the grill—steaks, fish, fajitas, quesadillas, low-fat veggies. It's a beautiful atmosphere."

Of an initial $1,443 dollar restitution order, he still owes about $900. "I intend to [pay it off]," he says. "I don't want to take anything to the street. . . . Once released from here, I'll have no paper on my head. I just want to continue working. . . . I don't need any more trouble. The world is full of it. It's so easy to get in, so hard to get out. Believe me, I've learned."

Boot Camps
"Motivated, Motivated, Motivated, Sir!"

THE INMATES at New York's Lakeview Shock Incarceration Correctional Facility, one of America's largest "boot camp" prisons, learn to speak only when spoken to, and to say "Sir" or "Ma'am," when they reply.

"Sir, yes sir," Reynaldo responds when asked if the six-month program he is about to complete has helped him any. His crisp white shirt and tie, his trim crew cut, and his disciplined bearing suggest that he has in fact come a long way from a life of hanging out and drug dealing in New York City.

That surprises him more than anyone else. He qualified for the program as a nonviolent offender facing a formidable three years to life for possessing a large quantity of cocaine. That's more than enough time to focus the mind of a twenty-year old. He figured he could fake his way through the rigors of boot camp for the chance to be released early. "I came to the program because I was told the program was six months, and [if] I complete it, I was going home," he explains.

Along the way, something happened. Even faked discipline requires one to do one's work, to sit still in class. "You start listening . . . and by just sitting there listening, you start getting it. You get interested in it, and then you start paying more attention."

Meanwhile, he began to feel better and stronger physically. "When I first came, I couldn't do even five push-ups. Now I can do fifty." And then one day, there was the epiphany.

"I realized I was wrong. . . . I thought I wasn't hurting nobody just because I was selling drugs. [I thought] if I don't sell it, somebody else is going to sell it. But I was wrong. I was hurting people's families. . . . I realized it was bad." He immersed himself in drug treatment sessions and came to terms with his own addiction; he studied and took the GED exam. Now, on the eve of his graduation from boot camp, he talks of going to college and finding a job.

"Sir, yes sir," he says again, affirming that the program turned out to be a good deal for him. And it could be a good deal for New York State as well: His six months in boot camp, rather than three years in prison, could save the prison system more than $60,000.

Many experts remain wary of such stories, and of the whole idea of boot camp corrections. The most heartfelt boot camp conversions may not survive the inmate's return to dysfunctional families and chaotic neighborhoods. And realizing prison cost savings depends on a shrewd balance of policy and practice that not all legislatures or corrections managers understand. Where it's achieved, however, the dividends are real and substantial.

American corrections' interest in military models dates back to the nineteenth century. The visionary superintendent Zebulon Brockway, for example, established a program based on military discipline and training at the Elmira reformatory in New York. Pictures from the era depict platoons of uniformed inmates on parade, drilling with fake wooden rifles, exercising en masse, and bending to their studies in an arithmetic class. The program also included a Swedish regime that prescribed steam baths, massages, and special diets to promote rehabilitation.

Such efforts eventually were discredited and abandoned, but men like Brockway at least believed in what they were doing. Modern correctional boot camps, also known as shock incarceration programs, sprang up in the 1980s for reasons that often had more to do with political marketing than sound correctional practice.

As tougher sentencing laws imposed unmanageable crowding on prison systems, states looked for ways to make early release of convicts more tolerable to an angry, fearful public. The typical boot camp enrolls young offenders sentenced to minimums of a year or more and allows them to gain freedom after only three to six months if they survive a demanding routine of work and military discipline in Spartan surroundings. They may also be required to make progress in substance abuse treatment, get a high school degree, or learn a job skill. Should they fail to meet the program's demands, they face imprisonment.

The idea proved saleable. Marching platoons and screaming drill instructors played well in the news media; as presented to the public, boot camps conjured images of Jack Webb or Clint Eastwood whipping groups of shiftless youth into fighting shape. They also recalled millions of Americans' own experiences with military training. Thus, by 1994 more than fifty boot camps were operating under the auspices of thirty-three states and the Federal Bureau of Prisons, for a total capacity of 8,255. The federal government guaranteed further expansion of boot camps by providing funds for them in the 1993 crime bill.

Today's correctional boot camp programs share common features: They generally accept only nonviolent offenders sentenced for a first felony, promising reduced prison time for those who graduate. Inmates wear uniforms and short haircuts and follow highly structured daily routines that include physical training, work details, and military drill.

In other ways, the programs vary. Capacities range from a few dozen in small states like New Hampshire and Wyoming up to more than a thousand in New York. Some offer a program lasting only 90 days, while at others it goes on for 120 or 180 days. Some are free standing while others are based on grounds of a conventional prison. And while some add on elaborate curriculums of substance abuse treatment, education, and job training, others stick to the basic military model.

Despite the boot camps' rapid spread and continued popularity with the public, some corrections experts and researchers now question their value. The military analogy, they point out, breaks down quickly once one gets only slightly beneath the surface. The purpose of military basic training is to instill habits of obedience and group loyalty that can mean the difference between life and death on the battlefield. Its relevance is less clear for people going back to individual lives in drug- and crime-ridden neighborhoods.

Doris MacKenzie and Dale Parent, two criminal justice researchers who studied boot camps for several years, make another point: "Basic training prepares soldiers for three to four years of military life, during which they are fed, clothed, sheltered, and given medical care, a job with chances of promotion and pay increases, and opportunities for continued education and training." If military service changes people for the better, they write, "it probably is due more to the period of extended support and structure than to six or eight weeks of basic training."

Furthermore, the harsh training style that resonates with the public no longer even has much relevance to the modern, all-volunteer military, which seeks out better-educated recruits for technically sophisticated tasks. To that extent, what goes on in many correctional boot camps is an anachronism, and in some cases an ugly caricature.

Josh Perry, a retired military policeman who now commands a school for prison-boot-camp drill instructors at Fort McClellan in

Alabama, shows his training groups news footage of an Ohio boot camp to illustrate how drill instructors should *not* behave. It begins with the drill instructors charging onto a bus full of inmates, roughly manhandling them out of it, screaming and cursing at them to move faster, grabbing stragglers, and smashing them against a fence for emphasis. Such scenes continue, interspersed with approving comments from a prosecutor and a judge.

"If a drill sergeant in the active army did any of those things," Perry says, "he'd be relieved and court-martialed. . . ." Whether in the army or in a prison boot camp, he says, "drill sergeants should be role models. They should be firm, fair, and impartial." Firm, he says, does not mean indulging in "harsh and tyrannical treatment. You say what you mean and mean what you say, and you can do that without resorting to cursing, spitting in people's faces, grabbing people's collars, and throwing them up against the fence."

"A lot of these kids," he adds, speaking of the inmates, "have seen more violence in their fifteen or sixteen years on earth than most people twice their age, so what are you trying to prove? Who are you trying to fool?"

A more central question, however, is whether boot camps, by whatever means, actually achieve their apparent goals of changing inmates' subsequent behavior and taking the pressure off crowded prisons. In search of answers, MacKenzie and Claire Souryal led an evaluation of boot camp programs in eight states.

They found that in all the states (Florida, Georgia, Illinois, Louisiana, New York, Oklahoma, South Carolina, Texas) offenders' attitudes grew more positive during their time in the boot camp. "They said that the experience had changed them for the better and that they were proud of themselves for being able to complete such a difficult program."

Even so, the researchers could find no evidence that the change reduced their rates of recidivism in any substantial way. In five states (Oklahoma, Texas, Georgia, Florida, South Carolina), they could detect no lower recidivism for boot camp graduates in comparison with similar samples of inmates paroled from conventional prison. In New York, boot camp graduates were less likely to be returned to prison for technical violations, but no less likely to be returned for new crimes. The Illinois and Louisiana graduates had fewer new crimes but more technical violations.

The disappointing recidivism rates prompt some states to establish "aftershock" programs for boot camp graduates back on the street. Arizona, for example, set up a "shock house" for those who have no jobs or stable housing lined up after release. Stan Fosdick, who administers the program, points out that in addition to chaotic homes and neighborhoods, boot camp graduates also have to deal with "old homeboys. . . . who are very threatened by these people when they come out. They see them clean, clean shaven, not doing drugs, and the first thing they want to do is suck them right back into the drug culture . . . because it would threaten their gang if they didn't do so."

In addition to housing, fellowship and support, the shock house offers job placement and other services. Conclusions about its effect on recidivism await further research.

As for the second main boot camp objective, reducing need for prison beds, the findings were somewhat more positive. Boot camps could yield significant savings in beds, MacKenzie and Souryal found, to the extent that they enrolled offenders who would otherwise have been punished with prison, as opposed to probation, and kept those offenders from being expelled or dropping out (and then serving out longer terms in prison) before graduation.

The most crucial issue may be how offenders are assigned to boot camps. Admitting too many who otherwise would have gone on probation could produce a net increase in use of prison beds as those offenders fail the boot camp program and then go to prison. The best way to avoid this problem, the researchers suggest, is to give corrections departments the power to assess inmates already sentenced to prison and divert them to boot camp before they serve their prison time. Leaving the decision to sentencing judges, they say, "makes it more likely that the program will be used as an alternative to probation rather than to prison because judges often search for a sanction that falls somewhere in severity between probation and prison. While this may not be an unreasonable use of the program, it will have the undesirable effect of 'widening-the-net' rather than shrinking it."

Beyond making sure boot camp offenders really would otherwise occupy prison beds, managers of the camps need to maximize the rate at which they complete the program. Graduation rates of the eight camps studied by MacKenzie and Souryal ranged from a low of 48 percent (Florida) to a high of 91 percent (Georgia). Retention depends on the care with which managers screen eligible inmates, identifying poor candidates for success before they can be admitted.

It also depends on the extent to which drill instructors and teachers are willing to overlook breaches of discipline and failures of physical training, military drill, and substance abuse treatment. The issue requires the shrewd balancing of discipline, reward, and forgiveness for a population that arrives with a heavy burden of physical, mental, and emotional problems. Some boot camp administrators find it useful to set up "recycle" or "restart" programs that stop the clock for slower learners and give them an extra week or two of remedial help.

MacKenzie and Souryal also found that bed savings rates are further complicated as the issues of enrollment and retention are affected by the length of the program (the longer the stay, the more chances to flunk out) and its size relative to the total prison population.

"The analysis of the impact of the program on prison bedspace savings revealed that carefully designed programs can reduce prison crowding," they conclude. "Clearly, the major factor influencing prison bed savings is whether the boot camp program targets prison-bound offenders."

Dale Parent, a senior analyst at ABT Associates, developed a simulation model to estimate the effects of boot camps on prison bed-space needs. It factored in the rate of real substitution for prison beds, the retention rate, the capacity, the length of the program compared with regular prison terms, and the rate at which reoffending boot camp graduates return to prison.

Like MacKenzie and Souryal, he concluded that the most important factor for prison crowding "is the probability that participants would be imprisoned if the boot camp did not exist." Specifically, he found that if entrants to a 200-bed boot camp with a ninety-day program have only a 10 percent probability of imprisonment, the camp will generate a need for 502 additional prison beds. The model assumes that 30 to 40 percent of inmates will either be dismissed from the program or withdraw from it voluntarily. "If their probability of imprisonment is very low to begin with," Parent writes, "in-program failures quickly accumulate into a sizable block of new inmates, most of whom would not have been in prison at all if the boot camp did not exist."

The exercise showed that for boot camps with typical rates of in-program failure and returns to prison after release, the probability of initial imprisonment would have to be about 80 percent simply for the program to have no impact at all on prison bed needs. Even so, Parent found, large boot camps that do enroll only prison-bound offenders (by giving corrections departments the power to divert them) can have a significant effect on prison crowding.

So the researchers' bottom line remains positive: Well-designed shock incarceration programs can reduce the need for prison beds. They do so in a way that the public will support and that, compared with prison, gives inmates some positive experiences that may bear fruit later on.

Michael is a burly nineteen-year old who landed an Arizona boot camp after violating probation and accumulating new aggravated assault, weapons, and drug possession charges. He

credits the program with helping him gain control of a wild temper and getting a new start on a calmer life committed to work
and his girlfriend, who is pregnant with his child.

"I was a real jock in high school," he says. "I became very
narcissistic . . . I got into fighting because we fought a lot at
home." At the boot camp, he says, the drill instructors are "in
your face, yelling and screaming and calling you worthless, just
pushing all your buttons to make you go out and control all
those things. . . ."

Eventually, he found himself flourishing, becoming the leader
of his platoon. "After you start getting physically fit, you just
start feeling better over all," he says. "My drug habit was gone .
. . and we had a good primary drill instructor, a Godly man. He
helped us in a lot of ways we never could have found in our-
selves. It helped us a lot."

He had faced a minimum of six and a half years. If not for the
boot camp, he reflects, "I'd be in prison or I'd be dead."

A two-ton concrete bulldog wearing a spiked collar and a drill
instructor's Smoky Bear hat stands guard at the entrance to the
Lakeview Shock Incarceration Correctional Facility. Inside, the
bulldog's face, designed a few years back by an inmate artist,
decorates walls, sweatshirts, and documents, a pervasive
reminder of the camp's commitment to toughness.

Ron Moscicki, a career correctional officer and Lakeview's
superintendent, is by now used to being asked if his own face
was the model for the bulldog's. He insists it wasn't, but the
question is reasonable. A beefy, compact man, he strides across
the camp's windswept yards looking for cigarette butts, litter, or
uncut grass—and is proud to say he rarely finds any. Even on
frigid winter mornings, he shows up in sweatclothes at the
"grinder," a concrete slab where inmates drill and exercise, for
5:30 workouts that start the day; he usually doesn't go home
until well into the evening.

As he worries about staffing, budgets, and disciplinary policies, he also keeps his eye on the details—insisting, for example, that water pitchers be positioned on dining tables with their handles facing in the same direction. "If I get staff and inmates worrying about water pitcher handles, they're going to worry about the big stuff," he says. "Our facility runs from the top down. It starts here."

And running it is no small job. Lakeview, located in the town of Brocton, some forty-five miles southwest of Buffalo, New York, is one of the nation's largest correctional boot camps, with 600 beds located at a sprawling new medium-security prison complex. The campus also houses 500 more inmates in various stages of reception for the boot camp program or awaiting placement out of it. New York runs two smaller camps, of 300 and 250 beds, at other locations, for a total boot camp capacity of 1,650, or 3,300 per year. Lakeview's population includes 180 females, making it the largest shock program for women in the country.

New York's boot camps opened in September 1987, after the legislature passed a law that envisioned "an alternative form of incarceration stressing a highly structured and regimented routine, which will include extensive discipline, considerable physical work and exercise and intensive drug rehabilitation therapy" in order to "build character, instill a sense of maturity and responsibility and promote a positive self-image. . . ." The program, operated by the New York State Department of Correctional Services, only enrolls offenders already sentenced to state prison. They are eligible if they are between sixteen and thirty-five, can be paroled in three years, are not convicted of a violent felony, a sex offense, or an escape, and if they have not previously been sentenced to felony time.

Those who qualify are further screened for medical and psychiatric problems and criminal histories that might raise doubts about their suitability. Boot camp managers have some discretion. "Say the guy's thirty-four-years-old now . . . and he stabbed a guy when he was sixteen, and there's been no [other] violence on his record . . . we'll let him in," Moscicki says. "If he stabbed a guy last year, we'll disqualify him." The goal, however is to accept as many as possible. About half survive the screening and are given the chance to volunteer for the program; only about 10 percent refuse to sign up.

The boot camp recruits' day starts in the dark, with reveille at 5:30 A.M. As lights go on, they jump out of bed to stand at attention in their cubicles. A wild scramble follows in the eight minutes they are allowed for washing, shaving, making their beds, and getting dressed. Then they form up as a platoon and march out for forty-five minutes of calisthenics on the grinder followed by a half-hour run around the compound.

They bellow "Sir, yes sir!" or "Motivated, motivated, motivated, sir!" as drill instructors demand to know if they are ready for a day of hard work. On the run, they chant in cadence: "I used to carry a .38 / But now I'm owned by New York State."

Lined up for breakfast, they stand in platoon groups at parade rest while waiting to pick up trays, then assemble at tables to eat in silence. They are allowed to take as much food as they want but required to eat all they take. No food remains to be scraped off plates as they file out for work assignments.

Inmate crews leave the compound by bus to cut brush along roads, clean up parks and beaches along Lake Erie, and perform other tasks for municipalities and public agencies. Those with "legal issues"—outstanding warrants or immigration problems that make them escape risks—remain inside the Lakeview compound to maintain the grounds, do custodial work, or go to shops where they learn vocational skills (a stone-masonry group fabricated the giant bulldog that greets visitors). Still others staff "Toys for Tots," sorting through donated boxes of damaged toys in order to salvage complete working models for distribution to poor children.

In the afternoon work stops and classes begin. Inmates change into white shirts and neckties to study basic literacy or prepare for the GED exam. (Those who already have high school degrees help to tutor others.) They also attend substance abuse treatment sessions, classes on "decision making," and platoon meetings. Lights go out at 9:30.

Platoons progress through stages of the program, signified by the colors of their hats, or "covers"—brown for the first two "zero" weeks, followed by green, then red, then yellow. To advance from one stage to the next, all the platoon's members have to pass tests on what they have learned so far. A stick with the platoon's flag, known as the "guide on," bears streamers for different areas of achievement; an inmate chosen as platoon leader carries the guide on when the platoon is on the march.

In addition to following the routine, inmates are expected to maintain "military bearing." As they move from place to place, they stand tall, walk in straight lines, and execute crisp turns. They stare straight forward at all times; too much "eyeballing" may earn a bad report and eventual discipline. For their six months in the program, inmates give up their own clothes for camp-issue uniforms; women as well as men are shaved nearly bald as they enter and may not let their hair grow out beyond a short crew cut.

They are allowed few personal possessions and have no access to television, weight rooms, sports, or other recreation activities. Phone calls are limited to one every two weeks, and while they may see visitors on weekends, the remoteness of the camp—a ten-hour drive from New York City—makes visits rare for many inmates.

Despite the austerity, however, anyone spending more than a few hours at the camp quickly realizes that the main focus is on help rather than discipline. Inmates spend 41 percent of their time on treatment or education, only 26 percent on physical training and military drill. (Work accounts for the other 33 percent.)

In drug treatment classes, inmates confess their histories of drug abuse and explore the way to recovery with counselors and with each other. The Alcohol and Substance Abuse Treatment program, known as ASAT, is based on the twelve-step recovery process.

Inmates also participate in a routine called Network that aims to teach responsibility for self, to others, and for the quality of one's life. It prescribes five steps to decision making for problem solving and greater self-esteem: See the situation clearly, know what you want, expand the possibilities, evaluate and decide, act.

Beyond teaching the five steps, Network informs the inmates' communal life. Platoons of fifty-four or more live together as units for the duration of the six months. Each evening, the entire platoon meets for Network community exercises: Inmates are singled out for criticism from others, either in the form of written notes or direct face-to-face confrontations. Under pressure from peers and counselors, they admit their faults and say how they will work on improving their relations with the rest of the group. Or they volunteer to discuss negative behaviors, like gossiping and badmouthing, and how to overcome them, usually by finding constructive ways to bring problems and conflicts out in the open.

Overall, Network and ASAT seem as pervasive a part of Lakeview's atmosphere as its military trappings. For every gung-ho slogan painted on a wall ("Who Dares WINS!") there is likely to be a listing of the twelve steps to sobriety or the five steps to decision making. The program's philosophy, also painted on the walls, begins with, "Shock is a positive environment for human development in a caring community where members can help themselves and each other. . . ." It is a long way, in other words, from Lakeview to the stereotypical basic training at a place like Parris Island.

The program's approach to discipline reflects the therapeutic community far more than the military. There are, to be sure, the summary punishments—pushups, moving piles of rocks— imposed on whole platoons for the infraction of a single member. But the program also takes some care to track inmates individually, and in some detail. They are evaluated daily on their performance in Network meetings, work, and drill and ceremony. Teachers assess progress three times per week, while ASAT counselors submit weekly reports. When negative comments pile up, an inmate is called before a "learning experience committee" that discusses infractions or lack of progress and imposes appropriate "learning experiences" as sanctions.

A typical case involves an inmate who, according to the staff report, is "constantly eyeballing, displays no self-discipline when it comes time for military bearing. Inmate has been counseled by staff and shows no progress." His punishment: to wear an "eyeball cover"—a baseball hat decorated with a bulging plastic eyeball—and write a 300-word essay on self discipline.

"The first thing about a learning experience," explains Brian Carroll, director of Lakeview's ASAT program, "is that it has to be something that can be done by the inmate. You can't say, 'Give me a thousand-word essay' if the inmate cannot read and write." Other learning experiences require inmates to wear sashes bearing words that describe their misconduct or negative attitudes. A more serious infraction—failure to follow orders, a violent outburst of temper—might result in a sentence to carry a heavy log or rock throughout the day. If two inmates get into a fight, they may be required to carry a long log together everywhere they go. The most serious violations are punished by the ultimate sanction: removal from the program to serve out one's original prison term.

Moscicki and Cherie Clark, the social worker who is director of shock development for the New York state prison system, make a point of their willingness to expel inmates who break the rules or who simply refuse to get with the program. "Graduating the wrong inmate to me is just as big a sin as throwing the right inmate out too soon," Moscicki says.

But they are also willing to show lenience. Only possession of a weapon, an escape attempt, or an assault on staff means irre-

versible dismissal. Other serious infractions may lead to confinement in a holding cell with the possibility of return to the program after a display of contrition, usually in the form of a letter
to the superintendent.

Over the years, Clark and Moscicki also developed devices to
help slow learners. Inmates who don't seem to catch on during
their first two "zero" weeks get a third week of orientation
where successful inmates nearing graduation offer tips on what
worked for them. And inmates who repeatedly fail evaluations
may be shunted into a "recycling" program where they are given
intensive ASAT classes. Of a sixty-person platoon, Moscicki
estimates, as many as fifteen may not graduate without a dose
of recycling.

The managers' investments of time and energy in reentry and
recycling hold the program's drop-out rate down to 37 percent
and contribute to the overall message: The bulldog may be
tough, but he also has a heart.

That idea comes through most strongly to many of the
inmates from the drill instructors, who eventually seem more
like supportive older brothers or sisters than martinets. Drill
Instructor, Wayne Lewis says that he finds himself counseling
members of his platoon "all the time." Especially in their early
weeks, he spends a lot of time persuading inmates overwhelmed
by the program's physical and psychological demands to stick it
out. "I don't let them quit," he says. "I tell them, once you get
here to me, you're not quitting. I don't want quitters." Helping
inmates through to the third month may make a crucial difference, since many don't begin to feel better about the program
and themselves until then.

"In the beginning, you do get upset with them," a twenty-
eight-year-old drug offender named Tommy says of his drill
instructors. But "by the third or fourth month, you come to see
that they're trying to help you. The drill sergeants are the best
persons to talk to when you have a problem." He says that he

went to his drill instructor when the stress of the program and separation from his family combined to make him feel like giving up. A man-to-man, heart-to-heart conversation persuaded him to keep going.

The program's emphasis on "a positive environment for human development" and "a caring community" runs so deep as to raise a fundamental question: If the boot camp is really just a big therapeutic community, does the military stuff have any value at all other than providing a tough-sounding cover for politicians, the media, and the public? Moscicki, Clark, and other staff members respond with strong arguments that, public relations aside, the military training is essential to making the treatment work.

"One reason our treatment piece is so good is not just the content," Moscicki says. It's that "the inmates sit down, they pay attention and they listen." Many who come to the camp have tried treatment before, he points out. "They've been through umpteen hundred groups . . . all these sit-in-a-circle, blame-it-on-your-mother-and-father [programs]. . . . What the military piece teaches them is that they can control their bodies, sit still, close your mouth, open your ears, and they listen. Once they know how to do that, the treatment piece takes hold, the education piece takes hold, and they get it."

In addition to whatever progress they make with drug treatment, he points out, the inmates also routinely show substantial gains in education, jumping an average of three-and-a-half grade levels over the course of six months—even though academics takes up only 13 percent of their time.

Inmates agree with the idea that military drill enhances education. Maribel, a thirty-one-year-old convicted of drug possession, says that because of the military training, "you have control of your mind." She considers her Lakeview ASAT experience far more effective than a New York City residential treatment program she had completed before her latest relapse and drug arrest. At Lakeview, she says, they "don't let you off the hook. They make sure it sticks in your head so that when you do go out there . . . you'll know what to do."

Carroll points out that the military discipline makes it possible for a single counselor to reach many more inmates than in traditional prison programs. "That's where the military bearing piece comes into play," he says. Referring to his years of drug counseling in conventional penitentiaries, he says, "you give me fifty-four inmates [there], and I'm in trouble. Here, I've got control already, so my job is ten times easier to get to them."

Other staff share his appreciation of the discipline that makes Lakeview and other boot camps a cleaner, safer work environment than traditional prisons. Beyond that, correctional officers consider the place a desirable assignment because "it's satisfying," says John O'Reilly, Lakeview's deputy superintendent for security. "You really feel like you're accomplishing something. . . . You see when the inmates first come in . . . they don't really care about themselves or anything else. And when they leave they have pride in themselves, they really care about doing something."

"If I was in real prison, I would be bored to death by now," Wayne Lewis says. "Because here you're doing something. In jail, you just sit there . . . housing inmates."

Not all staff members are so positive, of course. New York's unionized prison guards have negotiated the right to choose assignments based on seniority. Some choose Lakeview looking forward to the benign working conditions or perhaps just the chance to move close to home, not because they bring special skills to a boot camp staff. Moscicki copes with the problem by scrutinizing staff as closely as he scrutinizes inmates and coming down hard on those who don't share his passion for the program.

"I do meetings . . . with staff to curb the wild cards," he says. In one, he was "raising hell about the place being dirty" when a senior manager spoke up to say, "'but boss, every time you set the level, we get there and you raise the level.' I got ugly. . . . I said, `What's wrong with that? If you're talking like that, what does the guy running the unit say?'"

Each Thursday, a platoon graduates from one of New York State's boot camps. The staff convenes a ceremony modeled on that of a small private school or college. Families show up to watch as individual inmates are cited for special achievements and all are handed diplomas. Inmate honorees speak movingly about all they have accomplished and express their gratitude towards the instructors who stuck with them and made it all happen. Visitors are struck by the fact that time in a correctional program actually gave inmates the first taste of positive achievement many have ever known.

When Clark and Moscicki take their turns at the lectern, however, the mood turns darker as they express well-founded worries about the ability of even the most successful boot camp graduates to withstand the pressures of the real world. Those returning to New York City (but not those returning elsewhere) can take advantage of elaborate services designed to support the progress they have made at the camp as they become part of a special intensive supervision parole program.

They are followed by officers working in pairs, with caseloads of only thirty-eight per pair. The Center for Employment Opportunities enrolls jobless parolees in a training program, with pay, for up to seventy-five days, while the Vocational Development Program helps them find permanent work. The Fellowship Center provides individual and group substance-abuse counseling for six months after release, and the Episcopal Mission Society holds weekly meetings for boot camp graduates based on the Network program at Lakeview.

But the intensive aftercare operates only in New York City. And while Clark considers it crucial to the inmates' future, she is all too wary of the risks they face, the power of backgrounds that suddenly seem overwhelming when compared with six months in a treatment program. For many, it is families that pose the greatest threat, and she chooses to focus on that issue in her graduation speech. She commands the graduates to stand and orders a "left face." They pivot on their heels to confront the relatives sitting nearby.

"You take a look at those families," she says, "you think about what you're going to tell them about how they're going to celebrate with you . . . . You need to tell your family, `no, thank you' when they offer you a drink. You need to tell your family, `I don't do that anymore.'" In a few weeks, she asks, will they still be home, "or will you be hanging out somewhere? Or will you already be locked up?"

"I hate graduations," Moscicki says when it is his turn to speak. "Graduations worry the hell out of me. . . . I know that before you leave this property, before you put the key in the ignition . . . someone will go in the purse, in the glove compartment, in the trunk, under the seat and come out with something. And all this will go out the window like that."

They speak from sad experience. "Some of the families were sitting out there holding [drugs]," Clark says after graduation is over. "We've had families show up with beer bottles in their car, with coke in their purse. We've found stuff on buses, and we know."

The recidivism statistics so far don't provide much comfort. Between September 1987 and September 1994, 10,927 inmates graduated from New York's boot camps, while another 6,424 dropped out or were dismissed. The department examined rates at which graduates returned to prison for new offenses or parole violations up to five years after their release. For the first year, the figure was 10 percent; for the second, it increased to 30 percent, in the third it was 42 percent, in the fourth 53 percent and in the fifth 58 percent.

For the most part, the figures for boot camp graduates were better than those for comparison groups of convicts paroled from prison, but only by a few percentage points, and in the later years the gaps between boot camp and some comparison samples evaporate. A study of all those released from March 1988 to December 1990 found that 32.4 percent had been returned to prison by September 1994, compared with 38 percent of a similar group released from conventional state prisons in the same period.

Those are disappointing figures, given the heavy emphasis on drug treatment and personal rehabilitation and the investment in intensive parole supervision for graduates. Moscicki and Clark argue that the better comparison figures for the more recent years suggest that the program is improving its ability to change offenders for the better, but the validity of that assertion awaits further research.

There is no question, however, that the program saves the state substantial money. Boot camps cost $60.39 per inmate per day, compared with $51.86 in a minimum-security prison and $56.72 in medium security. But Department of Corrections officials calculate the average stay of inmates released from boot camps at 216 days, compared with 546 days had they not been diverted to the shock program and served out their time in prison. On that basis, the department estimates a net operating-cost saving to the prison system of $224.7 million for the 10,927 successful graduates between 1987 and 1994, a figure that takes into account the extra cost of boot camp days for the 6,424 who left before graduating.

The department estimates additional savings of $124 million as the cost of prison beds it did not have to add to the system because of the boot camp program and $5.9 million because of the reduced return rate of boot camp graduates. The overall saving for the first seven years of the program comes to $354.6 million.

Those kinds of savings permit boot camp managers to think more philosophically about recidivism and the overall value of the program. Giving inmates a positive experience, forcing them to come to terms with addiction and criminal behavior,

permitting them a taste of real achievement in wholesome surroundings looks like a good thing to do, however long its effects
may last.

"I keep telling people we're a hospital," Moscicki says. "If we
were a hospital, and you came to us because you had pneumonia, and we cured your pneumonia, we'd tell you . . . eat right,
exercise, take your medication and chances are you won't get
pneumonia again. But if you get pneumonia again, you don't
blame the hospital."

The Ladder of Sanctions
When Synergies Pay Off

KEVIN STILL isn't sure why they did it. Even though he kept messing up efforts to shake his addiction to drugs, the Maricopa County probation officers kept going to bat for him with the judges, recommending first this regime, then that one to keep him out of prison. He finally landed in a six-month residential drug treatment program run by the Salvation Army. That was the one that worked.

"I can't say what I responded to," Kevin says, pondering why the Salvation Army's take on drug treatment finally helped him into recovery. "It was just a good wholesome place." He marvels even more at the number of chances he was given—more, he figures, than he actually deserved.

His journey through the probation system in Maricopa County, Arizona, began in 1988 with an arrest for selling crystal methamphetamine to support his own addiction to the drug. The judge gave him four years of standard probation. That lasted for two years, until he started using again. When his urine showed up dirty, his probation officer charged him with a violation but persuaded the judge to reinstate him with a warning to stay away from alcohol as well as drugs.

Kevin kept using and stopped meeting probation appointments. That resulted in a second violation, but instead of prison, the judge extended his probation for three years and gave him a dose of work furlough—sixty days of overnights at the county jail while going out to his job during the day.

He continued using drugs and failed another test. Now the judge turned up the heat a bit more: a ninety day stretch on work furlough followed by intensive probation. On "intense," Kevin had to follow a schedule listing his whereabouts 24 hours per day, seven days per week, and if he wasn't going to be at home, at work, or meeting with his probation officer, he had to beg permission.

He was assigned a team consisting of a probation caseworker and a surveillance officer. When he met them for the first time, they saw the glaze of drugs in his eyes and demanded a urine sample. He sweated right there in the office for five hours wondering what to do. Finally, he admitted that he was using, figuring that now he was off to prison for sure. But instead of charging him with yet another violation, the caseworker told him that because he had been honest with her, she would allow him to enroll for thirty days of drug treatment.

The program booted him after twenty-one days because he wouldn't follow the routine or take it seriously. His caseworker had one more card to play: She immediately signed him up for the six-month residential program run by the Salvation Army.

There he finally settled down and began to work on the twelve steps. The clients paid their way by laboring in the group's enterprises around town. Kevin had experience as a warehouseman, so they put him to work in the storeroom where they keep clothing and furniture the Salvation Army collects for distribution to the poor.

Separated from his life of addiction for that much time, combining work with treatment in a group he found compatible, Kevin began to recover. When he completed the program, he moved in with his parents and found a new warehouse job. Before long he was promoted to supervisor, got his own apartment, bought a car and found a girlfriend. Now, he says, "Things are going good. . . . I've got money in the bank. . . . I'm paying my bills."

Having ascended the ladder of treatment and punishment, he's easing back down. His caseworker insists that he continue in outpatient drug treatment classes three times per week, a heavy demand on top of full-time work. He's not sure why he needs it anymore, but he's willing to go, if only out of gratitude.

"They kind of stretched it for me," he says of the county's intermediate sanctions system. "I'm glad they did."

To the judges and probation officers of Maricopa County, Kevin's case did not look like much of a stretch. The sprawling county that encompasses Phoenix and the surrounding desert valley is one of a few places in America where agencies have developed elaborate menus of programs that combine punishment and social service to fill the void between prison and traditional probation.

Typically, such programs order "laddered" sanctions according to toughness. The first rung of the ladder is standard probation; it is followed by some form of intensive probation supervision, then by house arrest with an electronic monitor, then by a requirement to report at a day center. Offenders who continue to violate rules may then be moved up to residential work-release or restitution programs and then to a boot camp before finally being sent to prison. Along the way, they can be required to enter outpatient or residential drug treatment programs as well.

Beyond easing pressure on prisons and jails and helping judges practice "tourniquet" sentencing—imposing tougher restrictions by increment—such systems produce real synergies.

Offenders like Kevin wind up getting the help they need to escape lives of drugs and crime. Probation officers, meanwhile, are able to take a more positive, creative approach to their clients, often finding success where once they might have found only more fuel for burnout.

In their 1990 book *Between Prison and Probation*, law professors Norval Morris and Michael Tonry argue the case for a comprehensive approach to sentencing that includes a range of sanctions more demanding than probation but less confining than prison. "We are both too lenient and too severe," the authors write. "Too lenient with many on probation who should be subject to tighter controls in the community, and too severe with many in prison and jail who would present no serious threat to community safety if they were under control in the community." Specifically, they call for greater use of fines, community service orders, and intensive probation supervision.

They look forward to the development of options that would make complex sentencing the norm: "For some offenders, a substantial fine may well be combined with an order that the offender make restitution to the victim, pay court costs, and be subject to a protracted period of house arrest, monitored electronically, for which too the offender pays the costs. For others, intensive probation involving regular and close supervision by a supervising officer playing a police role and also by a caseworker may be combined with a defined period of residence in a drug treatment facility, followed by regular urinalysis to ensure the offender remains drug free, and also an obligation to fulfill a set number of hours of community service. . . ."

They cited three reasons that justify incarceration: "to affirm the gravity of the crime, to deter the criminal and others who are like-minded, or because other sanctions have proved insufficient." They declared that "there are many in prison and jail who need not be there, who are at the shallow end of severity of crime and have criminal records that do not trigger any one of these selecting criteria. How many is a matter of guesswork." Prison officials, they say, estimate the number at 10 to 15 percent.

Criminal justice managers in some states have begun examining their prison populations with that in mind. In South Carolina, where the incarceration rate of 477 per 100,000 is 45 percent more than the national average of 329, Michael Cavanaugh coordinates a project to rationalize sentencing, expand the use of alternatives, and reduce the use of prison. Cavanaugh, former head of the state's Department of Probation, Parole and Pardon Services, points to a preliminary analysis of the prison population that shows nearly 15,000 admissions to prison in a three-year period on sentences of less than three years. These inmates, who accounted for nearly half of all prison admissions in that period, served an average of six months behind bars.

Cavanaugh's researchers also found many people on probation with current offenses and criminal records similar to those given the short prison terms. "There was no rhyme or reason" to the decisions about who went to prison and who stayed out, Cavanaugh says. He considers the pool of offenders sentenced to either probation or short prison terms the target population for a program of expanded intermediate sanctions. In the next phase of the project, the researchers will examine their cases to come up with a precise estimate of how many might safely and efficiently be diverted from prison.

The state of Texas took the process further. The legislature revised the penal code to require that violent felons serve at least 50 percent of their sentences, instead of 25 percent, before parole, but to prevent prison crowding, community programs were dramatically expanded for offenders deemed nonviolent.

The project was enacted under the administration of Democratic Governor Ann Richards, then reduced and restructured after Republican George Bush replaced her as governor in 1995 and scandal developed around contracting for treatment services. The idea of laddered sanctions continued at a regional level in Harris County, where the Community Supervision and Corrections Department developed an elaborate smorgasbord of refinements on probation supervision and residential programs. It included a restitution center, a boot camp, drug and alcohol treatment, and environmental conservation work. The programs got a financial boost from the judge supervising a lawsuit against the state prison system; he ordered money to the county for programs that could help reduce the prison population. But that set the county up for a loss late in 1995, when the judge found the state system in compliance, ending any need for court-mandated funding.

The state of Georgia may be the largest jurisdiction in America that has relied upon the laddered-sanctions idea for the longest time. Through the 1980s the Georgia Corrections Department's probation division created a ladder of eight different programs that give judges options other than prison for offenders who refuse to take probation sentences seriously. The Georgia schedule includes, in escalating order of toughness: regular probation, probation with special conditions, community service assignments, intensive probation supervision and house arrest, diversion centers (inmates work to pay restitution), probation detention centers (inmates live under higher security and do unpaid work for public agencies), and boot camps.

Thousands of offenders go through the programs each year. The residential programs—diversion centers, probation detention centers, and boot camps—have a daily capacity of 3,364 and handle about 10,700 offenders annually. Vince Fallin, associate commissioner of corrections, estimates that about half of them would go to prison if the programs weren't available. Thousands more per year are diverted to intensive probation, house arrest, and the other sanctions.

That's more than enough to take some pressure off the state's prison population, which currently totals 33,700. Though it has continued to increase as the intermediate sanctions have developed, Fallin points out that the increase is due mainly to fewer paroles; admissions to prison slowed with the expansion of the intermediate sanctions and actually began falling in 1993.

The turnaround occurred after probation and parole managers pointed to the high numbers of prison admissions for clients who had committed technical violations rather than new crimes. The legislature then passed a law mandating that first-time probation and parole violators be sentenced to one of the intermediate sanctions instead of prison.

Overall, the arithmetic conveys a powerful argument. "If we did not have all of these options," Fallin says, "we would be in dire straits in terms of prison beds."

Development of intermediate sanctions in Phoenix began in earnest with the arrival of Norm Helber, installed as chief of the Maricopa County Adult Probation Department in 1989. Recruited by Judge Michael Dann, then presiding judge of the county's Superior Court, Helber had been working as a county probation chief in New Jersey. He brought an eastern outlook to the conservative western state. At the time, the probation department offered only standard and intensive probation and supervised a work furlough program for inmates from the county jail. Basically, it was "either or; you place someone on probation or send them to prison," says Superior Court Judge Michael Ryan. "The judges were frustrated with being limited to that choice. There were certain people that had needs that could be addressed by something other than sending them to prison. . . and they didn't seem to pose a serious threat to the safety of the community."

"The judges really were frustrated about what was available to them in sentencing," agrees Dot Faust, the probation department's deputy chief for programs. "They weren't satisfied that anything was working that well . . . that the system wasn't behaving as a system."

The legislature had authorized a Community Punishment Program (CPP) providing for placement of certain offenders in drug treatment, sex offender therapy, or programs for the mentally ill, but it had not appropriated funds to begin operations. The CPP was originally conceived of as a form of probation enhancement, but as Helber arrived, lawmakers concerned about prison crowding decided to recast it as a prison diversion program and fund it with money shifted from the corrections budget.

Another development that fall also advanced the agenda. The National Institute of Corrections held its first national symposium on intermediate sanctions in Phoenix, focusing attention and stirring interest in the idea. The possibility of federal money and technical assistance aroused Helber's entrepreneurial instincts and intrigued the judges who ran the administrative office of the courts. They put together an intermediate-sanctions planning team to participate in the symposium and applied to make the county one of twelve national demonstration sites for intermediate-sanctions programs.

About the same time, the Vera Institute of Justice was looking for a place to test a program of day fines—the practice, well established in Europe, of setting fines according to an offender's earning capacity. The agency had developed a day fines program for misdemeanants in New York and sought a place to test the idea in a felony court. Vera and Maricopa officials came up with seed money for the program from federal and state agencies.

Helber and the judges turned their planning team into a formal steering committee that also included the county sheriff, prosecutor, and public defender, as well as county government officials. Helber, meanwhile, tinkered with probation itself, pushing for expansion of intensive supervision slots and creating specialized caseloads for sex offenders, the mentally ill, and spouse abusers.

As meetings of the steering committee brought all the players together, they realized how much they all had been acting as independent agents rather than working together for obvious efficiencies. The National Institute of Corrections (NIC) and a private Washington group called the Center for Effective Public Policy sent advisers to consult with Phoenix officials and facilitate meetings.

Helber recalls a major breakthrough in one session led by George Keiser of the NIC. He asked all the participants to state what advantages they saw for themselves in an intermediate-sanctions program. When it was time for Richard Romley, the county prosecutor, to speak, he said "absolutely nothing." The program, he explained, only created risk for his office, since it could get the blame if it agreed to an intermediate sanction for a person who then committed a new crime. "But I'll support it," Romley said, "because it's the right thing to do." His support would become crucial to promoting the program locally and in the state legislature.

Meanwhile, members of the team worked to educate judges, defense attorneys, and others about the benefits of intermediate sanctions and to involve them in details of planning. The day fines program, for example, requires that "units" assigned to individual offenses then be used to calculate actual fine amounts according to the offenders' earnings. "We let them sit down, judges and prosecutors as a team, and determine how many units of punishment [should be imposed for] any crime in our statute book," Helber recalls. "Once we did that, those who still had reservations . . . actually bought into the entire structuring of it, and then when it was implemented, they had a vested interest already."

A lawsuit challenging crowded conditions in the county jail gave the day reporting program a boost. Helber's people had used state funds to build three centers but lacked money to operate them. The centers, by enrolling inmates released early from jail, could reduce the ongoing need for 100 jail beds, Helber pointed out. Under pressure from the court, the county came up with operating funds.

Over the next few years, the team developed a ladder of 14 sanctions designed to offer combinations of punishment, incapacitation, and help, rendering the state penitentiary a last resort.

At the lowest level, offenders who pose no threat to the community and require little supervision—small-time white collar criminals, for example—are given traditional fines or day fines. Low-level offenders with drug problems may be referred to a drug court for court-ordered treatment. More serious offenders—drug dealers, thieves—are put on standard probation; sex offenders, spouse abusers, and those whose fall into certain other categories become part of specialized caseloads.

Offenders who would otherwise be prison-bound can qualify for the Community Punishment Program's regimes of drug, sex offender, or mental health treatment, under either standard or intensive probation supervision. Other prison-bound offenders may be placed on straight intensive supervision—house arrest.

More restrictive sanctions are based in the county's three day-reporting centers. The day reporting program enrolls youthful offenders and adult offenders released early from jail. Those subject to short jail sentences might be sentenced to thirty days of day reporting instead, under a program known as STEP (Short-Term Enhanced Probation).

At the next level, offenders are given split sentences consisting of a short time in jail followed by intensive or standard probation. Those in jail may be released during the day on work furloughs.

On a given day, some 23,000 people are on all forms of probation in the county; of these, Maricopa probation officials estimate, close to 2,000—about 1,000 in the Community Punishment Program and another 900 or so on intensive probation supervision—would otherwise be in state prison. In addition, the day reporting centers enroll about 200 on a daily basis, half of them offenders released early from the county jail.

The cost savings are significant. Arizona pays $48.64 per day to maintain an offender in state prison, while Maricopa County pays $40.40 per day for an offender in jail. The daily costs per offender of the Community Punishment Program, Intensive Probation Supervision and the Day Reporting Center are, respectively, $9.54, $11.70, and $18.68.

Even so, these efforts were not universally popular. As early as 1989, Sam Lewis, then Arizona's commissioner of corrections, fomented opposition to the Community Punishment Program in the state legislature, arguing that it had not diverted as many offenders from prison as the statute required even though funds had been shifted from his budget to pay for them in the community. A debate ensued over how to verify diversion; in the end the intermediate sanctions prevailed with credible numbers and the support of judges who saw their importance.

Still, the broader political climate in Arizona turned inclement for intermediate sanctions as the 1990s progressed. In 1992 Joe Arpaio replaced Tom Agnos as Maricopa County Sheriff. Agnos had served on the intermediate-sanctions committee and played an active role in the project; while Arpaio retained the seat, he argued loudly in public for the importance of putting criminals behind bars. By 1995 he was dominating the news of criminal justice in Phoenix and had attracted the attention of conservative politicians nationwide. "Every major newspaper and tv station in the world has covered me," he would boast. "Rush Limbaugh, Newt Gingrich, Phil Gramm—they continuously talk about me around the nation, and they do that for a reason."

The reason, in his view, was that "I want to put them in. . . . When someone violates the law, make sure there's room in jail. It's just a cop-out not to put people in jail."

To that end, he erected a tent city for 1,000 sentenced (as opposed to pretrial detainee) inmates. That called the bed-saving value of day reporting centers into question, since the tents now could accommodate sentenced offenders who had been overcrowding the jails. Probation officials point out that day reporting centers still could reduce demand for jail beds as inmates

who benefit from their programs—unavailable to occupants of
the tents—commit fewer crimes after their release. In any case,
the tent city, which quickly became notorious for both primitive
living conditions and lax security, hardly looked like a permanent solution and was likely to produce new court challenges.

Despite these frustrations, Helber and other supporters of intermediate sanctions in the county don't feel much threatened by all
the political posturing. The program is by now well established
and well appreciated by judges. On more than one occasion, the
probation chief points out, the ongoing committee that scrutinizes the system has proven its value. When a federal judge
leaned on the county to reduce jail crowding, for example, the
group produced a useful quick fix: assigning a few probation
officers to speed the processing of accused probation violators,
thereby lopping twelve days off the average time they spend
locked up pending hearings. That and the day reporting centers
quickly reduced the need for 500 jail beds, Helber says.

The most fundamental value of intermediate sanctions, however, may be the extent to which they allow so many criminal
justice officials to make better sense of themselves and their jobs.
"We can be smarter about punishment" thanks to the sanctions,
asserts Judge Dann. "It's important to help make punishments fit
crimes and offenders."

Thus Rena Glitsos, a county public defender, finds the Community Punishment Program useful. "I have had judges when
they sentence someone to probation with the Community Punishment Program actually say on the record, 'but for the Community Punishment Program, this individual would be going to
the Department of Corrections.'"

Abby Kennedy, a deputy county attorney, also sees its value.
"If you've got people who are hopeless drug addicts, and that
fuels whatever crime they do . . . and you keep sticking them in
prison for two years here, two years there . . . . they're going to

continue to reoffend, continue to be a drain on society, and that's where I'd much rather see somebody get drug treatment and then not have to prosecute them again."

Probation officers, on the front lines of the system, wax most thoughtful about its effects. Jerry Ott, a senior deputy probation officer, observes that before the expansion of intermediate sanctions, there was "more of an emphasis on playing the game 'I gotcha' with probationers. When I first started, some of the senior p.o.'s would actually take glee in catching somebody in the middle of messing up so they could take them back to court." And senior managers of the department encouraged that attitude.

Mark Stodola, who manages two of the day reporting centers in Maricopa County, recalls that when he started out as a probation officer, "the message that I received from supervisors was essentially, three strikes and you're out. . . . If somebody had three dirty u.a.'s, [urinalyses] you take them back to jail or recommend that they go to prison. It was just very, very punitive."

Today, he says, the priorities are reversed, with many probation officers working so hard to find alternative programs that they wear clients out. "The vast majority of people who I dealt with . . . who have gone to prison," he says, "have gone to prison because they said, 'I have had it with probation,' not because we said, 'we've had it with you.'"

Probation Officer Kathy Daniels appreciates the constructive interplay of punishment and social service under the new system. She talks about a probationer found to be using drugs and given a jail term as a condition of reinstatement. "He was in custody for awhile; then he was released to a day reporting center and that's when we started working on the other issues." Under the old system, "he would have probably been reinstated to probation with a jail term and would have just sat in jail. Then when the jail term ended he would have been back on standard probation without anything having been initiated."

In addition, she points out, the availability of so many sanctions has induced the department to formalize a staffing process for cases, forcing probation officers to think carefully about their decisions. Officers now meet with supervisors regularly to weigh the progress of each case, and it is common, she says, for an officer to present a case by saying, "This guy's had his chance. I'm going to wreck him in prison." After the group discusses the case, she says, the presenting officer may say, "That's a good point and maybe I'm being premature."

In the old days, she says, it was "easy to become angry at someone and say, 'Well, you've blown your chance. You just need to go to prison.' You . . . can't do that anymore. I think that's a good thing."

A forty-two-year-old former drug addict named Mike makes a good case in point. Over the course of three years on probation, he gave his officers plenty of reason for exasperation. Initially put on regular supervision for drug possession, he failed to show up for his first appointment with his probation officer. When police then arrested him, they found crystal methamphetamine in his pocket.

Instead of "wrecking him in prison" at that point, however, the probation officers suggested intensive supervision, then got him into the Community Punishment Program for outpatient drug treatment. That helped Mike to stay clean for a year and a half, until his mother died. "I got high for six days," he recalls. When his probation officer came by Mike told him, "I fell off; I'm getting high. I asked him to help me, and he said he would."

The officer brought Mike before a judge again with a recommendation that he be ordered into residential drug treatment for thirty days. "It was the best thirty days of my life," Mike says. His long-term drug addiction stemmed from traumatic experiences in Vietnam, but psychiatrists at the local Veterans Administration hospital told him long ago that there was nothing they could do to help. At the treatment program, however, he met a counselor who had "gone through the same kind of things I did" during the war. "He helped me understand things that had tormented me for years. . . . I never could talk about it before. . . . I hadn't even had a dream I could recall since 1970. . . ."

Since graduating from the program, he's dreaming again, not to mention working steadily as a truck driver and, with the help of a supportive girlfriend, staying drug-free. "These programs," he says, "have been able to structure everything back into my life—responsibility, and the ability and will to care."

Lessons
Defeating the Conventional Wisdom

EXPLORATIONS OF alternative sanctions commonly turn up promising examples of individual programs that work very well—along with broad-gauged research suggesting that most such programs succeed only minimally or fail miserably.

The skeptical research generally measures the quality of implementation more than the quality of the concepts themselves, yet the research nurtures a conventional wisdom that calls the concepts into question: Boot camps are dismissed as ineffective and counterproductive on costs—even though some boot camps work very well to save prison systems millions of dollars. Restitution gets dismissed as unworkable—even though well run programs are able to put offenders to work and collect huge amounts of money for restitution payments. Day reporting centers are condemned for "net widening"—even though carefully planned and managed programs achieve real reductions in prison and jail populations.

How do the successful programs, so often and so unfairly reduced to afterthoughts, defy the conventional wisdom? The answer isn't obscure. They are the programs that result from deliberate, intelligent planning, that receive adequate funding and human resources, and that enjoy the support of public officials who believe in the need for them. Yet the conventional wisdom makes those conditions hard to achieve. Skeptical public officials remain reluctant to spend time on intelligent planning, commit adequate resources or provide support and leadership. Then, rather than admit to poor implementation, they deny the value of the concepts themselves.

The preceding chapters, all documenting success of one sort or another, counter the skepticism. They make abundantly clear how much is possible where someone is willing to lead. Community service sentencing becomes a respected element of a city's criminal justice system, its clients a welcome presence in neighborhoods that benefit from their work. House arrest wins broad support as it saves taxpayers hundreds of millions in prison costs without generating any increase in crime. Business managers who rely on the restitution center for labor think about criminals—and their community's crime problems—in a new, more positive way. The potential of these programs is vast and all too often unfulfilled.

The stories of alternatives to prison also yield a number of more specific lessons:

1) While many programs successfully help offenders to rehabilitate themselves, recidivism shouldn't be the only measure of success.
Well-managed community service and restitution programs hold offenders accountable for crimes and extract payment for damages caused by criminal behavior. They impose humane punishment while supervising offenders in order to protect the public. And they may save on costs of incarceration in the bargain. Those benefits surely justify the use of such programs as a substitute for prison so long as offenders in them do not commit new

crimes at a greater rate than those who are traditionally incarcerated and released.

Managers of community service and restitution programs, and sometimes offenders themselves, talk about how the forced labor teaches work skills, sometimes the first the offenders have ever experienced. In a similar way, correctional boot camp inmates take pride in the self-discipline they acquire as they survive the rigors of military training, physical conditioning, work, and study. House arrest programs are believed to help some criminals and their families simply by forcing them to stay home and learn how to get along.

If research does not confirm that the experience helps them resist pressures to resume criminality after they serve their time, should that completely invalidate such programs? Only if it can be shown that using them as a substitute for prison either costs taxpayers more or exposes them to more crime. At a minimum, the programs produce savings, sometimes big savings, pose no new threat to public safety and teach some lessons that may one day prove valuable.

2) For all their promise, alternative sanctions remain vulnerable to the perverse complexities of social policy planning.

Programs hoping to put offenders to work so that they can pay restitution and fines, for example, find themselves hostage to local labor markets. Where few low-wage, low-skill jobs exist, the offenders may find themselves spending most of their time reading want ads and going for nonproductive job interviews. The program languishes as offenders grow frustrated and restitution goes unpaid. But where labor markets are strong, offenders quickly find paying jobs and victims receive promised restitution payments. In some cases, employers grow to depend on the new supply of drug-tested, court motivated workers for jobs otherwise hard to fill. Their support then gives the program political weight, cementing it in as a permanent part of community life.

In other cases, programs hang up on hidden administrative or conceptual snags. Intensive probation supervision intended to reduce the need for prison and jail cells may actually increase it as closer surveillance and more frequent drug testing turn up more violations of the rules. A correctional boot camp may create a big pool of new prison inmates as judges use it as an alternative to probation and offenders who flunk out land in prison.

Such problems need not be fatal to the programs. Designers of intensive supervision can build in other alternative punishments for technical violators; boot camps can recruit offenders after they are already sentenced to prison and they can take steps to hold down failure rates without diluting the rigors of the routine.

But promoters and managers of such programs need to remain aware of lurking dangers, building in the capacity for ongoing evaluation and revision. They also need to insist on enough time to work through implementation problems before critics proclaiming failure are allowed to destroy their efforts.

3) Scale is important.

Jurisdictions won't realize the practical benefits of alternative programs with only a token commitment to them. Suppose a court system sets up a program that orders offenders into residential drug treatment instead of prison. It succeeds famously, with a high percentage of offenders completing treatment, staying off drugs and out of crime. The program costs taxpayers $15,000 per offender per year, while a year in the state penitentiary costs $30,000. The program has a capacity of fifty, and its managers proudly claim that they are saving the state's taxpayers $750,000 per year in prison costs.

However much potential the drug treatment program represents in theory, it can't claim to save anything like $750,000 so long as it remains so small. For in fact it removes a negligible number of offenders from the state's prison population. No cell blocks are closed or not built because the program exists, no guards are laid off, no payrolls reduced.

The actual saving per client is no more than the marginal cost of keeping a prisoner for a day—meals, toiletries and the like. That might come to, by generous estimate, $4000 per year, or $200,000 for the fifty inmates. But the program requires a small staff to determine if inmates are eligible, keep track of their progress in treatment and take care of other administrative matters. Their salaries and expenses may easily equal or exceed the $200,000 prison cost saving.

The program can only begin to generate real savings as it grows to accommodate several hundred inmates per year, enough to warrant closing down whole wings of prisons or averting construction of new ones.

4) Such ambitions are justified

Where alternative sanctions are given the resources they need and are allowed to work, they easily prove their value, taking pressure off jails and prisons or making clear the potential for doing so. They give offenders the chance to turn their lives around, to the benefit of everyone. And they grant courts new flexibility to fashion sentences for individual offenders. No longer do judges face the dismaying choice of probation, where overworked officers provide little support or supervision, or sending offenders to chaotic prisons likely to return them to the streets more dangerous than when they went in.

But the issue is more than pragmatic. Alternative sanctions make it possible for law enforcement, courts and corrections to function together as a system, making rational use of costly resources. As important, they balance punishment with rehabilitation in a way that reinforces an ethical society's basic values. They allow communities to make sense of criminal justice.

Sources

Introduction

Publications

Anderson, David C. "The Crime Funnel." *New York Times Magazine*, 12 June, 1994.

Community Service

Publications

Committee on Criminal Justice Operations and Budget. *Community Service in the New York City Criminal Court*. New York: Association of the Bar of the City of New York, May 1992.

Krajick, Kevin. "Community Service: The Work Ethic Approach to Punishment," *Corrections Magazine*, 8 No. 5 (October 1982).

McDonald, Douglas C. *Punishment Without Walls: Community Service Sentences in New York City*. New Brunswick, NJ: Rutgers University Press, 1986.

McDonald, Douglas C. "Punishing Labor: Unpaid Community Service as a Criminal Sentence." *In Smart Sentencing: The Emergence of Intermediate Sanctions*, edited by James M. Byrne, Arthur J. Lurigio, and Joan Petersilia. Newbury Park, Calif.: Sage Publications, 1992.

McDonald, Douglas C. "Community Service Sentences." In *Intermediate Sanctions in Overcrowded Times*, edited by Michael Tonry and Kate Hamilton. Boston, Mass.: Northeastern University Press, 1995.

McDonald, Douglas C. "Community Service Sentencing in New York City." In *Intermediate Sanctions in Overcrowded Times*, edited by Michael Tonry and Kate Hamilton. Boston, Mass.: Northeastern University Press, 1995.

Organizations

Community Service Sentencing Project
Center for Alternative Sentencing and Employment Services
346 Broadway
New York, NY 10013-3971
(212) 732-0076

National Community Sentencing Association
c/o Myra Gaiser
Court Referral Program/Volunteer Center of Sonoma County
1041 Fourth Street
Santa Rosa, CA 95404
(707) 573-3399

Prisoners and Community Together (PACT)
254 Morgan Boulevard
Valparaiso, Indiana 46383
(219) 462-1127

Probation Services Division
Administrative Office of the Courts
Justice Complex CN 987
Trenton, NJ 08625
(609) 292-8925

Intensive Supervision Probation and House Arrest

Publications

Baird, Christopher, and Dennis Wagner. *Evaluation of the Florida Community Control Program*. Madison, Wis.: National Council on Crime and Delinquency, 1990.

Baumer, Terry L., and Robert I. Mendelsohn. "Electronically Monitored Home Confinement: Does It Work?" In *Smart Sentencing: The Emergence of Intermediate Sanctions*, edited by James M. Byrne, Arthur J. Lurigio, and Joan Petersilia. Newbury Park, Calif.: Sage Publications, 1992.

Baumer, Terry L., and Robert I. Mendelsohn. *Final Report: The Electronic Monitoring of Non-Violent Convicted Felons: An Experiment in Home Detention.* Submitted to the National Institute of Justice under grant number 86-IJ-CX-0041. Indianapolis, Indiana: Indiana University School of Public and Environmental Affairs, 1990.

Byrne, James M., and Linda M. Kelly. *Restructuring Probation as an Intermediate Sanction: An Evaluation of the Implementation and Impact of the Massachusetts Intensive Probation Supervision Program.* Final Report to the National Institute of Justice, Research Program on the Punishment and Control of Offenders under grant number 85-IJ-CX-0036, 1989.

Florida Department of Corrections. *Community Control "House Arrest": A Three Year Longitudinal Report, 1983–1986*. Tallahassee, Fla.: Florida Department of Corrections, 1987.

Florida Department of Corrections. *Community Control II (Continuous 24 Hour A Day Electronic Monitoring)*. Tallahassee, Fla.: Florida Department of Corrections, 1987.

Florida Department of Corrections. *Florida's Community Supervision Population Trends: A Summary of Trends over a Two Year Period*, January 1993 to December 1994. Tallahassee, Fla.: Florida Department of Corrections, 1995.

Petersilia, Joan, and Susan Turner. "Comparing Intensive and Regular Supervision for High-Risk Probationers: Early Results from an Experiment in California." *Crime & Delinquency* 36, January 1990, 87–111.

Petersilia, Joan, and Susan Turner. "Evaluating Intensive Supervision Probation/Parole (ISP) for Drug Offenders." *Crime & Delinquency* 38, October 1992, 539–556.

Petersilia, Joan, and Susan Turner. "Evaluating Intensive Supervision Probation/Parole: Results of a Nationwide Experiment." *Research in Brief*. Washington D.C.: National Institute of Justice, May 1993.

Petersilia, Joan, and Susan Turner. "Focusing on High Risk Parolees: An Experiment to Reduce Commitments to the Texas Department of Corrections," *Journal of Research in Crime and Delinquency* 29 (February 1992) 34–61.

Petersilia, Joan, and Susan Turner. "Intensive Probation and Parole." In *Crime and Justice: A Review of Research*, Volume 17, edited by Michael Tonry and Norval Morris. Chicago, Ill.: University of Chicago Press, 1993.

Petersilia, Joan, and Susan Turner. *Intensive Supervision for High-Risk Probationers: Findings from Three California Experiments*. Santa Monica, Calif.: RAND Corporation, 1990.

Petersilia, Joan, and Susan Turner. "Intensive Supervision Programs for Drug Offenders." In *Smart Sentencing: The Emergence of Intermediate Sanctions*, edited by James M. Byrne, Arthur J. Lurigio, and Joan Petersilia. Newbury Park, Calif.: Sage Publications, 1992.

Renzema, Marc, and D. T. Skelton. *Final Report: The Use of Electronic Monitoring by Criminal Justice Agencies, 1989: A Description of Extent, Offender Characteristics, Program Types, Programmatic Issues, and Legal Aspects*. Submitted to the National Institute of Justice, contract OJP-89-M-309. Kutztown, Pa.: Kutztown University Foundation, 1990.

Schmidt, Annesley K. "Electronic Monitoring of Offenders Increases." In *Research in Action*. Washington D.C.: National Institute of Justice, February 1989.

U.S. General Accounting Office. *Intensive Probation Supervision: Cost-Savings Relative to Incarceration*. Washington D.C.: General Accounting Office, 1993.

U.S. General Accounting Office. *Intensive Probation Supervision: Crime-Control and Cost-Saving Effectiveness*. Washington D.C.: General Accounting Office, 1993.

U.S. General Accounting Office. *Intensive Probation Supervision: Mixed Effectiveness in Controlling Crime.* Washington D.C.: General Accounting Office, 1993.

Organizations

Florida Department of Corrections
2601 Blair Stone Road
Tallahassee, Florida 32399-2500
(904) 488-5021

Georgia Department of Corrections
Floyd Building - Twin Towers E, Room 756
2 Martin Luther King Drive SE
Atlanta, Georgia 30334
(404) 656-4593
Community Corrections Division
(404) 656-4747

Region V Probation and Parole Services
4520 Oak Fair Boulevard
Tampa, Florida 33610
(813) 744-8555

Day Reporting

Publications

Curtin, Elizabeth L. "Day Reporting Centers: A Promising Alternative," *IARCA Journal,* (March 1990).

Curtin, Elizabeth L., and Jack McDevitt. *Massachusetts Day Reporting Centers.* Executive Summary submitted to National Institute of Corrections for grant number 89JO/GHEO. Washington D.C.: National Institute of Corrections, August 1988.

Mair, George. "Day Centres in England and Wales." *IARCA Journal* 9 (March 1990).

McDevitt, Jack, Glenn Pierce and Robin Miliano. *Evaluation of the Hampden County Day Reporting Center*. Boston, Mass. Crime and Justice Foundation, August 1988.

Parent, Dale G. *Day Reporting Centers for Criminal Offenders—A Descriptive Analysis of Existing Programs*. Prepared for the National Institute of Justice under contract number OJP-86-C-002. Washington D.C.: National Institute of Justice, September 1990.

Parent, Dale G., Jim Byrne, Vered Tsarfaty, Laura Valade and Julie Esselman. *Day Reporting Centers, Volume I: Summary Report*. Prepared for the National Institute of Justice under contract number OJP-94-C007. Washington D.C.: National Institute of Justice, September 1995.

Parent, Dale G., Jim Byrne, Vered Tsarfaty, Laura Valade, and Julie Esselman. *Day Reporting Centers, Volume II: Source Book*. Prepared for the National Institute of Justice under contract number OJP-94-C007. Washington D.C.: National Institute of Justice, June 1995.

Robinson, John J., and Arthur J. Lurigio. "Bringing Probation Back to its Roots: Community-Based Programs and Initiatives in Cook County." *IARCA Journal* 10 (March 1990).

Warwick, Kevin. "The Hampden County Day Reporting Center: the Final Phase in a Continuum of Community Reintegration of Inmates." *IARCA Journal* 18 (March 1990).

Organizations

Crime and Justice Foundation
95 Berkeley Street
Boston, Massachusetts 02116
(617) 426-9800

Hampden County Correctional Center - Day Reporting
325 Alabama Street
Ludlow, Massachusetts 01056
(413) 547-8000, ext2815

Hampden County Sheriff's Department
627 Randall Road
Ludlow, Massachusetts 01056
(413) 547-8000

Metropolitan Day Reporting Center
8 Kingston St.
Boston, Massachusetts 02111
(617) 753-6113

Drug Treatment

Publications

Anglin, M. Douglas, Douglas Longshore, Susan Turner, Duane McBride, James Inciardi, and Michael Prendergast. *Studies of the Functioning and Effectiveness of Treatment Alternatives to Street Crime (TASC) Programs.* Final report to the National Institute on Drug Abuse under contract number No1DA-1-8408. Washington, D.C.: National Institute on Drug Abuse, 1996.

Belenko, Steven. *The Arkansas Supervised Treatment and Education Program Court: Report on Implementation of Court Operations.* New York: New York City Criminal Justice Agency, 1994.

Belenko, Steven. *Comparative Models of Treatment Delivery in Drug Courts.* Washington, D.C.: The Sentencing Project, 1995.

Clines, Francis X. "Dealing With Drug Dealers: Rehabilitation, Not Jail." *New York Times,* 20 January, 1993.

District Attorney of Kings County. *Drug Treatment Alternative-to-Prison of the Kings County District Attorney: Fifth Annual Report of Operations, October 15, 1994 to October 15, 1995.* Brooklyn, N.Y.: District Attorney of Kings County, 1995.

District Attorney of Kings County. *Drug Treatment Alternative-to-Prison Project: Process Evaluation and Preliminary Research Report.* Brooklyn, N.Y.: District Attorney of Kings County, 1992.

Fisher, Ian. "Selling Addicts on Treatment Rather than Prison." *New York Times,* 1 December, 1992.

Goldkamp, John S., and Doris Weiland. "Assessing the Impact of Dade County's Felony Drug Court." In *Research in Brief.* Washington D.C.: National Institute of Justice, 1993.

Goldkamp, John S. *Justice and Treatment Innovation: The Drug Court Movement: A Working Paper of the First National Drug Court Conference, December 1993.* Final report to the National Institute of Justice under award number OJP-94-076M. Washington D.C.: National Institute of Justice, 1994.

Haaga, John G., and Elizabeth A. McGlynn. *The Drug Abuse Treatment System: Prospects for Reform.* Santa Monica, Calif.: RAND Corporation, 1993.

Hubbard, Robert L., Mary Ellen Marsden, J. Valley Rachal, Henrick J. Harwood, Elizabeth R. Cavanaugh, and Harold M. Ginzburg. *Drug Abuse Treatment: A National Study of Effectiveness.* Chapel Hill, N.C.: University of North Carolina Press, 1989.

Inciardi, James A., and Duane C. McBride. *Treatment Alternatives to Street Crime: History, Experiences, and Issues.* Washington D.C.: National Institute on Drug Abuse, 1991.

National Consortium of TASC Programs. *A Public Safety Partnership: The Criminal Justice System and Treatment.* Silver Spring, Md.: National Consortium of TASC Programs, 1995.

Simpson, D. Dwayne, and S. B. Sells, eds. *Opioid Addiction and Treatment: A Twelve-Year Follow-Up.* Malabar, Fla.: Robert E. Krieger Publishing Company, 1990.

Smith, Barbara E., Robert C. Davis, and Sharon R. Goretsky. *Strategies for Courts to Cope with the Caseload Pressures of Drug Cases.* Chicago, Ill.: American Bar Association, 1991.

Tauber, Jeffrey S. "Community Judging: A National Strategy for the Development of Coordinated Drug Court Systems." Paper presented to the United Nations Conference on Communities in the Global Drug Program, New York, N.Y., 1994.

Tauber, Jeffrey S. "Contingency Contracting in Oakland: Implementing Structural Accountability in a Drug Court Program." Paper presented at the National Association of Drug Court Professionals National Training Conference, Las Vegas, Nev., 1995.

Tauber, Jeffrey S. "Drug Courts: A Judicial Manual," *CJER Journal* (Summer 1994).

Tauber, Jeffrey S. "An Evaluation of the Oakland Drug Court After Three Years." Paper presented at the National Association of Drug Court Professionals National Training Conference, Las Vegas, Nev., 1995.

Turner, Susan. "Background Characteristics of Participants in the UCLA/RAND Study of Treatment Alternatives to Street Crime (TASC)." Paper presented at the annual meeting of the American Society of Criminology, Miami, Fla., November 1994.

U.S. General Accounting Office. *Drug Control: Treatment Alternatives Program for Drug Offenders Needs Stronger Emphasis*. Washington D.C.: General Accounting Office, 1993.

Vera Institute of Justice. *Studying the Differential Effects of Legal Coercion on Drug Treatment Retention*. Unpublished. 1994.

Young, Douglas, Denise Corcoros, and Timothy Ireland. *Diverting Drug Offenders to Treatment: A First Year Report on DTAP Expansion*. New York: Vera Institute of Justice, 1993.

Young, Douglas, Denise Corcoros, and Timothy Ireland. *Diverting Drug Offenders to Treatment: Year Two of DTAP Expansion*. New York: Vera Institute of Justice, 1995.

Organizations

Criminal Justice Program and Drug Policy Research Center
RAND
P.O. Box 2138
Santa Monica, California 90407
(310) 393-0411

Drug Treatment Alternative to Prison
Office of the District Attorney of Kings County
Municipal Building
Brooklyn, NY 11201
(718) 250-2231

National Association of Drug Court Professionals
901 North Pitt Street
Suite 300
Alexandria, Virginia 22314
(703) 706-0576

National Consortium of TASC Programs
8630 Fenton Street
Suite 121
Silver Spring, Maryland 20910
(301) 608-0595

New York City Criminal Justice Agency
52 Duane Street - 3rd Floor
New York, NY 10007
(212) 577-0500

UCLA Drug Abuse Research Center
1100 Glendon Avenue
Suite 763
Los Angeles, California 90024
(310) 825-9057

Sex Offender Treatment

Publications

Alexander, Margaret A. "Sex Offender Treatment: A Response to the Furby, et al. 1989 Quasi Meta-Analysis II." Paper presented at the conference of the Association for the Treatment of Sexual Abusers, San Francisco, Calif., 1994.

Bays, Laren, Robert Freeman-Longo, and Diane D. Hildebran. *How Can I Stop? Breaking My Deviant Cycle: A Guided Workbook for Clients in Treatment.* Brandon, Vt.: The Safer Society Press, 1990.

Bays, Laren, and Robert Freeman-Longo. *Why Did I Do It Again? Understanding My Cycle of Problem Behaviors: A Guided Workbook for Clients in Treatment.* Brandon, Vt.: The Safer Society Press, 1989.

Berlin, Fred S., Wayne P. Hunt, H. Martin Malin, Allen Dyer, Gregory K. Lehne, and Sharon Dean. "A Five-Year Plus Follow-Up Survey of Criminal Recidivism Within a Treated Cohort of 405 Pedophiles, 111 Exhibitionists, and 109 Sexual Aggressives: Issues and Outcome." *American Journal of Forensic Psychiatry* 12, No. 3, (1991): pp. 5-25.

Berlin, Fred S., H. Martin Malin, and Sharon Dean. "Effects of Statutes Requiring Psychiatrists to Report Suspected Sexual Abuse of Children." *American Journal of Psychiatry* (April 1991): 148:4, pp 449-453.

Borzecki, Mark, and J. Stephen Wormith. *A Survey of State-Run Sex Offender Treatment Programs in the United States*. Ottawa, Can.: Minister of Supply and Services,1987.

Donnelly, Sheila, and Roxanne Lieb. *Community Notification: A Survey of Law Enforcement*. Olympia, Wash.: Washington State Institute for Public Policy, December 1993.

Furby, Lita, Mark R. Weinrott, and Lyn Blackshaw. "Sex Offender Recidivism: A Review." *Psychological Bulletin* 105, No, 1, (1989): pp. 3-30.

Freeman-Longo, Robert, and Laren Bays. *Who Am I and Why Am I in Treatment? A Guided Workbook for Clients in Evaluation and Beginning Treatment*. Brandon, Vt.: The Safer Society Press, 1988.

Goode, Erica. "Battling Deviant Behavior." *U.S. News & World Report*, 19 September, 1994: 74–75.

Laws, D. Richard, ed. *Relapse Prevention With Sex Offenders*. New York: The Guilford Press, 1989.

Lieb, Roxanne, Janie Maki, and Peggy Slavick. *A Summary of Recent Findings from the Community Protection Research Project*. Olympia, Wash.: Washington State Institute for Public Policy, February 1994.

Marques, Janice K., David M. Day, Craig Nelsonn and Mary Ann West. "Effects of Cognitive-Behavioral Treatment on Sex Offender Recidivism: Preliminary Results of a Longitudinal Study." *Criminal Justice and Behavior* 21, No. 1 (March 1994): 28–54.

Marques, Janice K., David M. Day, Craig Nelson, Michael H. Miner, and Mary Ann West. *The Sex Offender Treatment and Evaluation Project: Fourth Report to the Legislature in Response to PC 1365*. Sacramento, Calif: California Department of Mental Health, October 1991.

Marques, Janice K., Craig Nelson, May Ann West, and David M. Day. "The Relationship between Treatment Goals and Recidivism among Child Molesters." *Behavior Research and Therapy* 32, No. 5 (1994): 577–588.

McGrath, Robert J. "Sex Offender Treatment: Does It Work?" *Perspectives* (Winter 1995): p.p. 24-26.

Mussack, S. E., L. Person, and C. Thomas. "Methodologies for Extinguishing Deviant Sexual Arousal and Deviant Sexual Fantasies Within a Community Based Treatment." Unpublished.

Nordheimer, Jon. "Vigilante Attack in New Jersey Is Linked to Sex-Offenders Law," *New York Times*, 11 January, 1995.

Peterson, Iver. "Mix-Ups and Worse Arising from Sex Offender Notification." *New York Times*, 12 January, 1995.

Pithers, William D., Georgia Cumming, Linda Beal, William Young, and Richard Turner. "Relapse Prevention." In *A Practitioner's Guide to Treating the Incarcerated Male Sex Offender*, edited by Barbara K. Schwart. Washington D.C.: National Institute of Corrections, 1988.

Pithers, William D., Gary R. Martin, and Georgia F. Cumming. "Vermont Treatment Program for Sexual Aggressors." In *Relapse Prevention with Sex Offenders*, edited by D. R. Laws. New York: The Guilford Press, 1989.

Popkin, James, Gareth G. Cook, Ted Gest, Joseph P. Shapiro, and Mike Tharp. "Natural Born Predators." *U.S. News & World Report*, 19 September, 1994: 65–73.

Solicitor General of Canada. *The Management and Treatment of Sex Offenders*. Ottawa, Can.: Solicitor General of Canada, 1990.

Organizations

Association for the Treatment of Sexual Abusers
10700 Southwest Beaverton Hillsdale Highway
Suite 26
Beaverton, Oregon 97005-3035
(503) 643-1023

Safer Society Foundation
P.O. Box 340
Brandon, Vermont 05733
(802) 247-3132

Vermont Center for Prevention and Treatment of Sexual Abuse
P.O. Box 606
18 Blair Park Road
Williston, Vermont 05495
(802) 879-5620

Washington State Institute for Public Policy
The Evergreen State College
Seminar 3162
Olympia, Washington 98505
(360) 866-6000 ext. 6380

Residential Restitution

Publications

Bazemore, S. Gordon. *The Restitution Experience in Youth Employment: A Monograph and Training Guide to Jobs Components.* Washington D.C.: Office of Juvenile Justice and Delinquency Prevention, September 1989.

Department of Probation, Parole, and Pardon Services. *Report to the South Carolina Legislature: Comprehensive Community Control System.* Columbia, S.C.: Department of Probation, Parole, and Pardon Services, April 1994.

Hudson, Joe, and Burt Galaway. "Restitution Program Models with Adult Offenders." In *Criminal Justice, Restitution, and Reconciliation* edited by Burt Galaway and Joe Hudson. Monsey, N.Y.: Willow Tree Press, 1990.

Lawrence, Richard. "Restitution as a Cost-Effective Alternative to Incarceration." In *Criminal Justice, Restitution, and Reconciliation*, edited by Burt Galaway and Joe Hudson. Monsey, N.Y.: Willow Tree Press, 1990.

Schneider, Anne Larason, Shumway Warner, and Jean Shumway Warner. *National Trends in Juvenile Restitution Programming.* Washington D.C.: Office of Juvenile Justice and Delinquency Prevention, July 1989.

State Reorganization Commission. *An Evaluation of the South Carolina Department of Probation, Parole, and Pardon Services' Restitution Center Program.* Columbia, S.C.: State Reorganization Commission, November 1991.

State Reorganization Commission. *A Follow-Up Evaluation of the South Carolina Department of Probation, Parole, and Pardon Services' Restitution Center Program.* Columbia, S.C.: State Reorganization Commission, December 1993.

Weitekamp, Elmar. "Restitution." In *Intermediate Sanctions in Overcrowded Times*, edited by Michael Tonry and Kate Hamilton. Boston, Mass.: Northeastern University Press, 1995.

Weitekamp, Elmar. "Restitution in Philadelphia." In *Intermediate Sanctions in Overcrowded Times*, edited by Michael Tonry and Kate Hamilton. Boston, Mass.: Northeastern University Press, 1995.

Organizations

Department of Probation, Parole, and Pardon Services
2221 Devine Street, Suite 600
Columbia, South Carolina 29250
(803) 734-9220

Georgia Department of Corrections
Floyd Building - Twin Towers E, Room 756
2 Martin Luther King Drive SE
Atlanta, Georgia 30334
(404) 656-4593
Community Corrections Division
(404) 656-4747

Boot Camps

Publications

Clark, Cherie L., David W. Aziz, and Doris L. MacKenzie. "Shock Incarceration in New York: Focus on Treatment." *Program Focus*. Washington D.C.: National Institute of Justice, August 1994.

Cowles, Ernest L., and Thomas C. Castellano. *"Boot Camp" Drug Treatment and Aftercare Intervention: An Evaluation Review*. Washington D.C.: National Institute of Justice, July 1995.

Mackenzie, Doris Layton. "Boot Camps—A National Assessment." In *Intermediate Sanctions in Overcrowded Times*, edited by Michael Tonry and Kate Hamilton. Boston, Mass.: Northeastern University Press, 1995.

MacKenzie, Doris Layton and Dale Parent. "Boot Camp Prisons for Young Offenders." In *Smart Sentencing: The Emergence of Intermediate Sanctions*, edited by James M. Byrne, Arthur J. Lurigio, and Joan Petersilia. Newbury Park, Calif.: Sage Publications, 1992.

MacKenzie, Doris Layton, and James W. Shaw. "The Impact of Shock Incarceration on Technical Violations and New Criminal Activities." *Justice Quarterly* 10, No. 3, (September 1993): 463–487.

MacKenzie, Doris Layton, James W. Shaw, and Voncile B. Gowdy. "An Evaluation of Shock Incarceration in Louisiana." *Research in Brief*. Washington D.C.: National Institute of Justice, June 1993.

MacKenzie, Doris Layton, and Claire Souryal. "Multisite Evaluation of Shock Incarceration." In *Research Report*. Washington D.C.: National Institute of Justice, November 1994.

New York State Department of Correctional Services. *The Sixth Annual Shock Legislative Report*. Albany, N.Y.: New York State Department of Correctional Services, 1994.

New York State Department of Correctional Services. *The Seventh Annual Shock Legislative Report*. Albany, N.Y.: New York State Department of Correctional Services, 1995.

Parent, Dale G. "Boot Camps Failing to Achieve Goals." In *Intermediate Sanctions in Overcrowded Times*, edited by Michael Tonry and Kate Hamilton. Boston, Mass.: Northeastern University Press, 1995.

Organizations

Lakeview Shock Incarceration Facility
P.O. Box T
Brocton, NY 14716-0679
(716) 792-7100

New York State Department of Correctional Services
Director of Shock Incarceration
220 Washington Avenue - Building 2
Albany, NY 12226-2050
(518) 457-8144

Rehabilitation Training Instructors Course
U.S. Army Military Police School
Fort McClellan, Alabama 36205-5000
(205) 848-4483

The Ladder of Sanctions

Publications

Byrne, James M., Arthur Lurigio, and Joan Petersilia, eds. *Smart Sentencing: The Emergence of Intermediate Sanctions.* Newbury Park, Calif.: Sage Publications, 1992.

Clear, Todd R., and Anthony A. Braga. "Community Corrections." In *Crime,* edited by James Q. Wilson and Joan Petersilia. San Francisco, Calif.: ICS Press, 1995.

Maricopa County Adult Probation Department. *Desk Reference to Intermediate Sanctions in Maricopa County.* Phoenix, Ariz.: Maricopa County Adult Probation Department, 1994.

Morris, Norval, and Michael Tonry. *Between Prison and Probation: Intermediate Punishments in a Rational Sentencing System.* New York: Oxford University Press, 1990.

Tonry, Michael, and Kate Hamilton, eds. *Intermediate Sanctions in Overcrowded Times.* Boston, Mass.: Northeastern University Press, 1995.

Organizations

Georgia Department of Corrections
Floyd Building - Twin Towers E, Room 756
2 Martin Luther King Drive SE
Atlanta, Georgia 30334
(404) 656-4593
Community Corrections Division
(404) 656-4747

Harris County Community Supervision and Corrections Department
Courthouse Annex 21
49 San Jacinto Street
Houston, Texas 77002
(713) 229-9561

Maricopa County Adult Probation Department
P.O. Box 3407
Phoenix, Arizona 85030
(602) 506-3261

DATE DUE

NO DUE			

DEMCO 38-296